*God Did Not
Ordain Silence*

God Did Not Ordain Silence

by
Christopher J. Christianson

LOGOS INTERNATIONAL
Plainfield, New Jersey

All Scripture quotations are taken from the Revised Standard Version of the Bible unless otherwise indicated. Used by permission.

GOD DID NOT ORDAIN SILENCE

© 1974 Logos International, Plainfield, NJ 07060
All Rights Reserved
Printed in the United States of America

Library of Congress Catalog Card Number: 73-84157
ISBN: 0-88270-054-5 (paper)
      0-88270-069-3 (cloth)

Dedicated to
the Honor and Glory of God,
the Father, the Son, and the Holy Spirit

*God Did Not
Ordain Silence*

Chapter I

I CANNOT RECALL what first prompted me to think about *listening* to God. It may have been a sermon I heard, or something I read. It may have been a combination of several things, which is often the way the Lord convinces us to do something, or to believe something. He has a way of deliberately juggling the laws of chance.

A person may "happen" to read something in a book. Then he "happens" to hear someone mention the same thing. Then he "happens" to read a passage in the Bible that mentions the same thing. The next Sunday the pastor "happens" to mention this same subject, too. As one young man put it, "I think the Lord is trying to tell me something."

God does speak. The Bible is filled with indications; "And God said," "God spoke," and "Thus says the Lord," appear hundreds of times in Scripture. The first chapter and the last chapter of the Old Testament reveal that God speaks, as do the first and last chapters of the New Testament. The Bible begins and ends on the note that God is not a silent God.

And God still speaks today. He tells us in Scripture, "I the

Lord do not change." He still carries on His part of the conversation. It is only that people do not listen to Him.

One day, several years ago, as I stretched out in our reclining chair for a catnap after lunch, I heard a voice say, *God did not ordain silence.* I had not begun to doze, having barely started to relax when the voice spoke. I heard the voice clearly. It was distinct and abrupt. And audible. But no one else was in the room.

At first I was puzzled and prayed for enlightenment. It was too easy to interpret a supernatural message to mean what one wanted it to mean, like the Israelites of old who interpreted so much prophecy the wrong way.

The true meaning of that statement gradually became clearer to my mind. One day, as I prayed, an inner voice informed me, *As a loving Father, I want to speak to My children, but they do not listen to Me. Tell My people to listen, for I would speak with them.*

As a young teenager, I had never even thought about listening to God. I had simply said my prayers every night as I had been taught. I was deeply disturbed by the discrepancy between what the church taught about creation and what science theorized. The thought would start churning in my mind, that if there isn't a God, then there is no life after death, and, if there is nothing beyond this life, none of my family who meant so much to me would ever again exist. The idea of eternity without God was overwhelming. And sometimes, I would feel the tears of hopelessness trickle from the corners of my eyes.

My usual posture in prayer was to lie on my back in bed with my hands folded across my chest. I had noted at several funerals in my youth that this was the normal position of corpses in caskets. Naïvely I assumed this was the position in which the people had died. Uncommonly afraid of death, I normally prayed by enumerating my requests, followed by the Lord's prayer and then the prayer taught to me in early childhood,

"Now I lay me down to sleep." I always hurried over the part, "and if I die before I wake," because I wanted to be sure I got my hands unfolded before I fell asleep.

I was not an agnostic; I was a Christian who very much wanted to believe. When I left home at the age of eighteen to enlist in the Marines, I continued my religious practices. But I longed for more assurance of the reality of God.

World War II was in full swing when I started to attune my inner ear for divine communication. Our Marine brigade was stationed on Guadalcanal in the South Pacific. We were using the island as a training and staging area for future campaigns. We had seen action in the Marshall Islands and on Guam, and now we were preparing for another invasion. Where? We would find out when the time came.

It was difficult then, and still is, for me to attune my inner hearing. My usual practice was to read a portion of Scripture and say my prayers each night after I had crawled into my bunk, using a flashlight if the lights went off before I finished my reading. After I had said my prayers, I would make a decided effort to be perfectly still in obedience to Psalm 46:10: "Be still, and know that I am God." To me, this meant that in quietness and confidence I could experience the reality of God, and so I relaxed my body and tried to make my mind void of any thought. Sometimes it helped to imagine myself with a broom, sweeping all thoughts from my mind. And I did find that, with practice, I could gain some control over my unruly thoughts.

My main problem was being too sleepy. I came to the conclusion that bedtime was a poor time to say my prayers, because even without falling asleep, in a drowsy condition a person sometimes says things he doesn't intend. Once, as I was praying the Lord's prayer, I was startled to realize I had just prayed, "*My* kingdom come, *my* will be done on earth . . ."

The most meaningful periods of meditation in those early

days were the occasions when I found relaxation on the beach. Our camp was situated in a coconut grove bordered by the jungle on one side and the Solomon Sea on the other. I would find a quiet place along the beach where the coconut trees afforded some relief from the tropical sun. As I lay there, the gentle lapping of the waves and the cooling balmy breezes had a soothing effect on my whole being. The rhythm of the waves seemed like the heartbeat of the warm earth beneath me, and I wanted personally to know the Creator of this universe.

In this relaxed condition, I tried to converse with God, but praying was hard work for me at that stage in my life. Heavily encumbered with the ingrained awkwardness of the King James' vocabulary I had grown up on, I prayed brief prayers, and then paused for a short while to allow God an opportunity to say whatever He might want to say. Often thoughts came to me that seemed reasonable answers to my questions, but I didn't actually hear a voice of any kind.

This was an experimental thing, one I did not pursue on a regular daily basis. Nevertheless, although I received no vocal replies, I remember the distinct feeling of peace and general well-being that permeated my mind, and the inspirational thoughts I received.

It was around this same time that I started tithing. I am not certain what caused me to do it, though there was no question that it was a clear principle in the Bible. I mention this, not because I believe it is a prerequisite to fellowship or communication with God, but simply to indicate what was happening to me at that particular time in my life.

It was in the same period that I also sensed an urge, or slight nudge, toward the ministry. Previously, I had thought of many things I would like to do, but I had never, even for a moment, thought of being a pastor. For this reason, I believed the urge must have come from God, and I asked the Lord if He truly wanted me in the ministry. I had not yet learned to attune my ear to God's still small voice, but I had heard of another way of letting God speak to an individual.

A Christian friend had told me how he allowed God to answer his requests for guidance. He would pray earnestly about a problem for which he sought direction. Then he simply asked God to answer him through His Word, the Bible. Holding his Bible in such a way that it would fall open by itself at random, with his eyes closed, he would place his finger on one of the opened pages. Whatever verse or passage his finger indicated, he considered God's answer to him.

One afternoon when I was alone in the pyramidal tent we called home in those days, I could stand the dilemma no longer and determined to settle it. After all, I was soon going to be twenty-one, which was pretty old for a man not to know where he was going in life. Did God really want me to be a pastor? I prayed earnestly, for school had never particularly appealed to me. But if God truly wanted me to study for the ministry, I was willing to do it. Then I simply asked God to show me His answer through His Word. I allowed my Bible to fall open, and plunked down my finger. When I opened my eyes, my finger rested on Timothy 3:1 (KJV): "This is a true saying, If a man desire the office of a bishop, he desireth a good work."

I had no idea how to figure the laws of chance, but I was aware that my finger could have pointed to any of the thousands of verses that would not have had any relevance to my prayer. Momentarily the thought came into my head that I ought to try once more just to double-check, but I dismissed the idea, not wanting to do anything to jeopardize this precious experience.

From that moment on, I pondered the possibility of entering the ministry with new interest, though I hadn't the slightest idea what a pastor did other than preach on Sunday and visit a few sick people.

What I had really wanted to be, ever since grade school days, was an inventor. As a young teenager I had researched patent possibilities of some gadgets I had thought up. I received some encouragement, but had never gone ahead with any actual patent applications. Only a few weeks before praying about the ministry, I had received a book in the mail that listed many needed inventions. I pored over its pages, jotting down ideas and making rough sketches of proposed inventions.

The pastorate would be all right, if that was what God wanted. But I earnestly loved the field of invention, and so one night, I attempted to make a deal with God. I told Him that I would be willing to give my afternoons to the ministry if He would let me spend my mornings at my workbench.

Very distinctly and very loudly I heard an unequivocal *No!* It was so loud that I was sure the others in the tent had heard it, too. It taught me that the creature does not make deals with the Creator. God initiates the covenants, not man.

The answer to that prayer had the effect of instantly intensifying my interest in listening to God. I knew that He could speak so I could hear Him.

On the following Sunday, as I was leaving the chapel worship service, the chaplain handed me a *Link* magazine. He had seen me attending the services regularly, but he didn't know my name or anything about my interests or problems—at least on the human or conscious plane. Even so, I did notice that he hadn't handed a magazine to the man ahead of me or the man ahead of him. And as he gave the magazine to me, he said, "Perhaps you'll find something of interest to you in here."

Back at my tent, I opened the magazine. The very first article I turned to announced, "Not everyone should be a minister." It explained that God entrusted some people with the ability to make large sums of money, and the Lord needed such men to support the work of the Kingdom through their donations.

This put me in a quandary. Did God want me in the ministry, or did He want me to follow my desire of inventing things? I had read that some inventors had made great fortunes.

Did God want me only to provide special income for His Kingdom work?

Looking back to that period of frustration in my life, I can see clearly what troubles so many earnest Christians today: they want to know God's will for their lives. They are not so concerned with having their own way blessed of God, as they deeply desire to know exactly what it is God wants them to do. How often I have heard Christians express this torment, "If only I knew for sure what God wants of me!"

In my search for God's answer, I had found at least three ways that He could communicate with me. I had received an answer through the use of my Bible; I had heard the audible voice of God; and I had received direction through another person or incident (the chaplain handing me a magazine).

Since receiving the Lord's tender and gentle instruction, *Tell My people to listen, for I want to speak with them,* I have endeavored to make people aware of the two-way communication of prayer.

I once heard of two boys who found an abandoned mine shaft about a mile from their homes. The shaft was fifteen feet deep, and only one short exploratory tunnel led from it. The boys converted the old mine into their own private hideout. They built a crude ladder down the shaft, and scavenged discarded pieces of furniture to make a cozy retreat for themselves in the mine tunnel. Finally, they rigged an old stove pipe to serve as a means of communication from the tunnel to the surface, through which they hollered messages to one another on occasion.

One day the weathered old shaft collapsed, trapping the boys in the mine. It was useless for them to try to dig out through the tons of rock and earth. They took turns yelling up the stove pipe, not knowing if it was still intact or if anyone might be within earshot. After a short while, their kerosene lantern flickered and went out. The boys huddled together in the damp darkness. At intervals they took turns hollering into the stove pipe until their voices became hoarse. Finally they concluded, "What's the use? No one is listening anyway." And they quit yelling up the pipe.

(This story represents the prayer experience of all too many people. How often people say, "Oh, I tried prayer. But it didn't seem to work.")

Many hours passed. The boys were cold and hungry. They were tired, and they were scared. Leaning against each other, eventually they fell asleep. Some time later, they awakened. Something had aroused them; they didn't know what. Nor had they any idea of the time other than that by now, surely their families would be looking for them.

Then they heard a faint noise filtering down through the stove pipe. New hope surged through them, and they listened breathlessly. Faintly they heard someone calling their names. Excitedly, they both began hollering up the stove pipe. They *knew* someone was there.

Many Christians honestly believe that "Prayer pays," and that "Prayer is power," but eventually become discouraged when it seems they are merely hollering through a pipe with no one listening at the other end. But the moment people hear something from the other end, their interest in prayer is renewed and their faith is strengthened. Prayer truly is a two-way communication, and God wants to speak to His children.

Chapter II

I HAD NOT been able to find a definite solution to my dilemma concerning the ministry before our outfit, now grown to division strength, moved out from Guadalcanal.

Our troop transport left Guadalcanal on March 15, 1945, its compartments crammed with more than 2,000 battle-ready Marines, its holds filled with war matériel, and its deck covered with trucks, jeeps, and landing craft battened securely for the long sea journey. Several similarly loaded sister ships accompanied us, and there were a few small destroyer escorts deployed on the periphery of our convoy. As the trip progressed, other ships of all sizes and descriptions joined with us.

The bunks of the troop compartments were stacked so closely together that one had to decide whether he wanted to sleep on his back or on his stomach before he slid into his bunk; there wasn't room to turn over. In the humid tropical waters, the crowded troop quarters perpetually smelled like a locker room after a game. Several of us slept topside, under the trucks on deck, whenever the weather permitted.

When we were well at sea, our company was called to a

meeting on the ship's fantail where we were informed of our destination—Okinawa, the main island in the Ryukyu group, just 300 miles from Japan—and briefed on the enemy troop strength and probable displacement.

When the meeting broke up, there was little of the usual lighthearted joking and friendly jostling. Most of the Marines moved slowly away, looking for a small private spot to sort out their thoughts about this strange island on the enemy's doorstep.

To me, the uppermost concern was why in heaven's name had they scheduled the assault landing for April 1, Easter Sunday morning? Somehow, I felt, it must have something to do with the Sunday surprise Japan had dealt us at Pearl Harbor. Perhaps they figured the enemy wouldn't expect us to make our assault landing on a Sunday, especially not on Easter Sunday.

I couldn't help feeling it was an insult to the Lord. In those days I felt particularly close to Him, and after the brief, well-attended communion service on Easter eve, I prayed about this matter at some length. I felt a need to apologize to the Lord for making our assault landing on Easter morning. And as heavy casualties were anticipated, I particularly asked the Lord to watch over and protect us on this special day. I listened then, but heard no reply, although a sense of peace did settle over me.

Reveille sounded at 0400 on Easter Sunday. We could hear the continuous rumble of heavy naval gunfire as we hastily ate a hearty breakfast of steak and eggs, our last fresh food for no one knew how long. After wolfing it down, we hurried up on deck to watch the action.

The first light of dawn was edging along the eastern horizon. There were dark silhouettes of ships everywhere, of all sizes and descriptions. It was the largest armada ever assembled, eclipsing even D-Day, the year before. Battleships and cruisers were hurling their heavy artillery onto the beachhead. Carrier-based planes were dive-bombing fortifications along the coast and around the Yontan airbase, the first important objective of our Sixth Marine Division. Some Japanese planes approached our huge fleet, but they were shot down, and none of the ships that I could see were hit.

At 0630, the bosun's whistle shrilled over the ship's public-address system: "Now hear this. Now hear this. All Marines report to your compartments to await orders for disembarking. All unauthorized personnel must go below."

Unhurriedly, the Marines went to their assigned compartments to don their gear. I was an infantry radioman, a member of a communication team called a shore party. It was our special task to go ashore in one of the first waves of landing craft and establish radio communications between shore and ship, and between the various combat units and division command. So, besides our normal combat gear, we also had to carry our radio equipment ashore.

There was the usual good-natured banter going on among the men of our party. No one listening to our conversation would have guessed that we were about to make an assault landing. One buddy complained, "I completely forgot to shave this morning."

"You'd better pray they don't hold an inspection as soon as we get to the beach," came the reply.

And someone else volunteered, "I'd let you shave with my stiletto, but I don't want to dull the blade."

At our debarkation stations, we descended three abreast down the Jacob's ladders into the waiting Higgin's boats that bobbed like corks on the jostling waves. We bounced around for almost two hours while the boats jockeyed into their proper positions at the line of departure, much like racehorses getting lined up at the starting gate. Again I asked the Lord for His protection, and took heart. The extraordinary peace I felt had not left me.

At last the signal was given, and our wave headed for the beach. The boats grated to a halt a quarter of a mile offshore on an underwater coral reef. We stepped off the boat ramp—into waist-deep water. Several Marines lost their balance, and those who managed to stay upright gave assistance to the others.

Wading across four hundred yards of jagged coral reef to get to the beach, we were sitting ducks for enemy machine-gunners and snipers. It was then I became aware of something absolutely incredible: the awesome silence around us. Sure, we could hear the big guns and planes in the distance, but it was as if someone had turned off the sound track up close. This was my fourth assault landing, and something was missing: where was the clatter of enemy machine guns and the zip of snipers' bullets? The whump and geysers of water from their mortars?

Once I thought a buddy of mine had been hit. He gave out a yell and disappeared beneath the water. I rushed over only to learn that he had stepped into a man-size hole in the coral reef. He was completely soaked, equipment and all, but otherwise okay. We quickly learned there were many such potholes and even cavernous-sized openings in the coral reef, and we began watching those ahead of us; as long as they didn't disappear beneath the water, we followed in their tracks. And so we came ashore in long lines, instead of the usual broadside attack—unbelievably vulnerable. A single machine gun could have wiped out a whole company. Only there were no machine-guns at all.

The moment we got to the beach, we set our radio up and sent the electrifying message: "Enemy has abandoned this area of island."

Within two hours, our division had captured Yontan Airfield, which had been designated the objective for the third day. The few Japanese we did find were quickly overcome, and our heavy equipment and supplies came pouring ashore hours ahead of schedule.

I thanked God that night for a miracle.

Each successive day we encountered heavier enemy opposition. The northern end of Okinawa, which was assigned to our division, was mountainous terrain of extravagant beauty. The hillsides were terraced and gave a general appearance of a huge, well-tended Japanese garden. But these hills were honeycombed with caves, trenches, and tunnels skillfully designed by the enemy to completely command every approach, every valley, while having his entire force and operation hidden underground. A quiet, pastoral hillside, seemingly devoid of any enemy installations, could, in fact, contain an entire battalion, with barracks, mess hall, hospital and gun emplacements so skillfully concealed in a network of tunnels that even through field glasses, one could not see even a hint of enemy activity. They, on the other hand, could watch every move we made through small gunports which were carefully camouflaged among shrubbery and trees.

Each morning our command post received reports from all of the attack units. The daily number of killed, wounded, and missing mounted, but even so, our casualties were much lighter than those sustained by the enemy. In less than three weeks, our division had overcome all organized resistance in the northern two-thirds of the island.

And then it began to rain, and it poured almost non-stop for seven days. During that water-logged week, we had to move our troops and our caravans of vehicles to the south. By this time I had been assigned a radio jeep, as the chief of a radio team of five men. As there was room for only two men and their gear in the jeep, three of our men had to ride in one of the trucks.

The torrential rain turned the heavily used road into a stream of gooey brown clay. For a time we could inch along in four-wheel drive, but in places the mud was two feet deep—too much even for the doughty little vehicle that was designed to go anywhere. We soon had to intersperse the jeeps between huge trucks which could then push them through the mire whenever they bogged down. By the time we arrived at our new location in the south, the spare wheel on the back of our jeep had been rendered completely useless by the massive bumper of the troop transport behind us.

Units of our division moved right into the hot and heavy battle. The Japanese had an observation post on the Shuri Heights, where they monitored every move we made. They had carefully coordinated and calibrated the entire island so that they could direct their artillery and mortars with pinpoint accuracy.

One evening, just at dusk, Lieutenant Bittle told me to get my radio jeep fueled and ready, and to pick one of the men from my team to accompany me on a special mission. He also told another team chief to get his jeep ready and to pick a man to assist him. We were told to report to Colonel Worthington at the commissary the next morning at 0530.

I asked the Lieutenant, "What sort of a detail is this, do you know?"

"I wasn't told," he replied, "but I would guess it's to establish ship-to-shore communication for unloading food supplies."

Jaros, the other team chief, suggested, "I'll flip you to see who gets to go aboard ship."

After six weeks of combat rations, eating aboard ship sounded like an invitation from the King who gave a wedding feast for his son. Jaros flipped the coin into the air and called, "Heads!" He caught the coin and quickly slapped it onto his left wrist. As he slowly lifted his fingers, his face fell: tails.

The next morning the four of us reported to Colonel Worthington at 0530. The Colonel asked who was going out with him, and I indicated that Becker and I were the lucky ones. The Colonel told us to drive our jeep aboard the armored amphibious vehicle. Then the ramp was raised, and the tractor crawled out to sea. We waved back to the others, shouting, "Don't wait supper for us."

Becker checked out our frequency with Jaros' radio. Our code name was Warhorse, and they were Red Dog. About ten minutes after we had set out to sea, the Colonel said, "You guys better put on your tin hats." We sat bolt upright, surprised. "Why?" I asked.

Colonel Worthington said, "Our wave is starting toward the beach."

A couple of days earlier our division had reached the Asa

Kawa Estuary. A footbridge had been built across the river, and two of our battalions had gotten across before a Japanese suicide team rushed the bridge and blew it with a satchel charge. The Marines who had gotten across the river were somehow able to keep their meager toehold, and had even made some headway, a few inches at a time. But the enemy's fortifications and troop concentrations were such that our dive-bombers and rocket planes could do little to soften them. What was needed was tanks and heavy artillery. To accomplish this, it was necessary to establish a new beachhead south of the estuary, and drive a wedge inland far enough to allow our engineers to build a bridge for our heavy equipment.

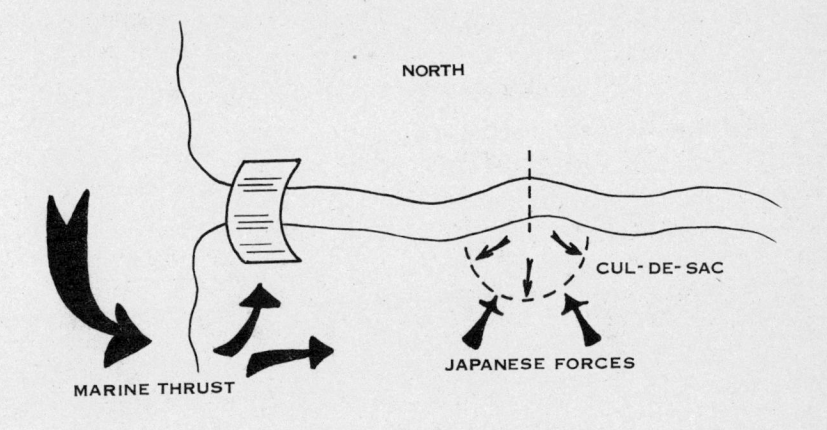

With only a few minutes' warning, Becker and I became part of that beachhead. We could have been court-martialed for leaving our helmets, rifles, and packs back at headquarters. We had thought we were going aboard a ship. We wouldn't have needed such things there. Colonel Worthington was an understanding officer, and he told us to requisition equipment off the first casualties we found. That didn't take long; there were plenty of casualties right on the beach. Our radio was the only communication between our beachhead and the command post that was now established back at the commissary. Each time we sent a message, the Japanese lobbed mortar shells onto the beach in an effort to knock out our radio, and we had to keep moving.

By noon the fight had moved inland, and the beach was relatively quiet. But whenever we would send another radio message, a new round of mortar shells would come in with their whirring sounds. Finally Colonel Worthington said, "You boys better close up shop. Your radio is attracting too much fire. Don't break radio silence until I tell you to."

The orange ball of the sun was just sinking into the western sea when the Colonel returned to the beach after holding conferences with his field officers. His face showed the strain of battle as he approached the jeep with a message in his hand. "You'll have to break radio silence. Get this off to Red Dog right away."

"Shall we keep moving as we send the message?" I asked.

"I think you're safe enough here," he said. "We've pushed their mortars back quite a ways."

Our jeep had been parked behind an embankment all afternoon. Quite a number of reserve troops were now sitting around behind the same embankment, eating their evening rations.

Our troops had not reached their planned objective, and the attack would have to be continued the following morning. However, our units were almost out of ammunition, and our urgent message requested fresh supplies of ammunition, mortar shells, and grenades. After Becker had sent off the message and received an acknowledgment from Red Dog, he became nervous. He was twenty-six, which in the Marines was an old man. What's more, he was married and had two children. He still had his earphones on and held the microphone in his hand when he slapped my arm and said, "Let's get out of here! Just in case."

I had just gotten comfortable and was inclined to sit tight, but something inside made me heed him. We cranked up and had gotten fifty feet down the beach when three mortars exploded directly behind us.

Colonel Worthington approached our jeep again. "Man alive, are you lucky!" he said. "There were a dozen casualties over there." He pointed toward the embankment we had just left.

After another month of intense combat, the entire island was secured, during which members of our signal company were called on to take the place of fallen comrades in the forward observer teams for directing naval gunfire and air-ground liaison teams for spotting targets for dive-bombers and rocket planes.

The enemy troops were surrendering in droves toward the end. Four of us guarded three hundred prisoners confined in a stockade consisting of a single strand of barbed wire. Our prisoners could have crawled under it, or stepped over it, but they were content to sit in squatting fashion until they were interrogated and sent on to other detention camps. There were no incidents of any kind. Our prisoners were polite and obedient. I found I had a deep compassion for the Japanese. Even to this day I sense a special love, a special concern for them.

The one hundred days I spent on Okinawa left a deep impression on my life. There was the Easter miracle. That's the only way I can describe it. Had it not been for that miracle, not one in ten would have made it to the beach as we slowly waded ashore on the coral reef. Then, too, the dozen casualties from the mortar fire intended to knock out our radio at the Asa Kawa beachhead made me determined to make my life count for something.

Finally, the tremendous cost of war grieved me, especially the cost in lives. This was indelibly impressed upon my mind on July 4, 1945—just ninety-five days after our division first set foot on Okinawa—when I attended the dedication ceremony of the Sixth Marine Division Cemetery. Situated on a hillside overlooking the Yontan landing beaches and the East China Sea, the cemetery contained row upon row of neat, white crosses and Stars of David over the graves of 1,697 of our fellow Marines who had died in the capture of the island. And this was the toll of just one of the five divisions of soldiers and Marines who fought on Okinawa.

The dedication ceremony that day included prayers by three chaplains—Protestant, Catholic, and Jewish. As the service concluded with the haunting notes of a bugler playing taps, the tears streamed down my cheeks. How many grieving families are represented by these crosses and stars, I thought. How much poorer is our world because of all these lives cut so short!

Shortly after the island was secured from the Japanese, our division embarked for Guam where our rest camp had been set up. Here we were to prepare for our next campaign: the invasion of Japan itself.

One evening during August, 1945, the fellows in our tent were reminiscing about some of our close buddies who had died on Okinawa. Many of them had been wonderful guys, the kind you'd want your sister to marry. We talked about the young lives that had been snuffed out, and we shared what we had known of their hopes and dreams. My heart ached for the families and friends of my dead pals. Still vivid in my mind's eye were the horribly pulped bodies of two of them, and the white, cold feet of a third protruding from beneath a camouflage poncho.

My heart was heavy that warm August night as I crawled into my bunk, securely anchoring the green netting around me for protection against the tropical mosquitoes.

At bedtime, the master switch was always pulled, shutting off all the electricity for our camp. I read my Bible by flashlight as usual. I am no longer certain what passage I read, but I will never forget my prayer.

I spoke to God from the depths of my heart about my burden.

I spoke of how terrible I felt about all the inhumanity, the brutal killing and horrible suffering, the senseless expenditure and waste of war, the utter futility of war as a means of settling disputes between nations. Then I prayed that if it were somehow possible for me to undertake some special mission that could end the war, I was willing to do it—even if it meant losing my life.

The moment I prayed that prayer, I was enveloped in a marvelous peace, that "peace which passes all understanding." I was at perfect peace with God, at peace with myself, and at peace with all people everywhere.

Nor was it gone in the morning; in fact, all the next day I basked in that strange and wonderful peace. I felt an aura of expectancy. At every moment, I felt someone would tap me on the shoulder and tell me exactly what special mission I was to undertake.

But nothing happened that day that involved me in any unusual way. That night, everything followed the usual customary routine.

After the lights and radio went off, I read my New Testament and had just started to pray when suddenly I heard men shouting in the distance. Moments later, the lights came on, and the radio returned to life. The news was electric: the United States had dropped a new type bomb on Hiroshima, and Japan had sent a message to Switzerland that she was ready to sue for peace.

This came as a great surprise, and we were ecstatic. We had been thinking about nothing but the invasion of Japan, and the oft-repeated warning was that the United States would suffer no less than a million casualties in the coming campaign. It took a gigantic shift in our conditioning in those few moments to realize the significance of the news.

I was as joyous and excited as the next fellow, but deep in my inner being I was restless. The thought was gnawing within me that I had offered myself to God as a sacrifice. But now the idea haunted me that perhaps God wanted the total sacrifice all right, but a living sacrifice for some special purpose. That idea stuck in my mind like a burr in a wool sweater. I just could not shake it. And I tried; I was willing to do whatever God wanted of me—if only I knew for certain what He wanted.

The war was soon officially ended. Two months later I returned to the States, and a month after that I was discharged, quite appropriately, on Thanksgiving Day, 1945.

Upon returning home, I immediately went to work in a local ice cream factory. Dad had been a salesman for them and had been killed in one of their trucks, in an accident on sleeted highways shortly after I had enlisted in the Marines. My older brother was in North Africa with the Army at the time. My older sister was a stenographer in Minneapolis, but she soon enlisted in the Waves. My younger brother was injured in the same accident that took my Dad's life, but he recovered and later joined the Navy.

Our family was born and raised in the Lutheran Church. All my life I had automatically attended worship services every Sunday morning with my family. I was third in our family of eight children. Mother was church organist, and Dad had sat next to the center aisle with us kids taking up the rest of the pew. As each of us was confirmed, we had graduated from the pew to the choir loft, and from the choir loft we were launched into the world.

Our family had always been close-knit. People watched when our car parked at the curb beside Trinity Lutheran Church in Blue Earth, Minnesota, and they stared in wonder as all ten of us climbed out, dressed in our Sunday best. It was never discussed whether or not we should attend worship. We always did, and that was that.

My postwar job with the ice cream factory required that I work six ten-hour days a week for two weeks, and then six nights for two weeks, and every other Sunday I had to work from eight in the morning until early afternoon. Soon I found myself debating whether or not to attend worship on the Sundays when I didn't work.

I still cared deeply about spiritual things, but, from a very human point of view, I was perpetually exhausted. About the time I got accustomed to sleeping in the daytime, it would be time to shift back to working days. My schedule was continually changing back and forth, and I seemed to average only about five hours of sleep at a time. So it wasn't unusual that on alternate Sundays I often decided to sleep. My family seemed to understand and accept my situation.

It wasn't long before I was seldom in church. I did, however, keep in touch through participation in the youth program and choir rehearsals, and I continued to tithe.

I had been caught up in this work-oriented life for several months when one autumn Sunday the Lord began interfering with it. When I arrived home from work early that afternoon, the rest of the family had already left to attend the annual youth rally and choral union in the town of Elmore about ten miles away. These rallies were held each fall and were attended by the youth and the choirs of many of the Lutheran churches in the neighboring communities. My mother had played the accompaniment for the combined choirs at that event for many years.

The afternoon session was scheduled to begin at three o'clock, followed by a choir rehearsal before the dinner hour. The finale came in the evening with the big rally and concert. I had told my mother that I planned to attend if I didn't have to work too late.

But my heart wasn't attuned to attending a church rally, and there was a movie showing downtown that I wanted to see. I showered and dressed, and started to walk. Two blocks from my home was a highway intersection. One highway led downtown, the other to Elmore. God was sharpening my conscience as I approached that intersection that day. I stopped at that corner and wondered what I should do. I finally decided to flip a coin. Heads, I would go on downtown to the movie; tails, I would hitchhike to the rally. I flipped the coin. It was tails.

Reluctantly, I crossed the intersection to hitch a ride. I barely had gotten my thumb out when a car stopped for me. In it was a young couple going, not only to Elmore, but to the rally.

When we arrived, the afternoon business session of the Luther League had just adjourned. Two of my friends who had attended the meeting came bursting out of the parish hall. When they saw me, they put their arms across my shoulders and moved me toward the auditorium where the choral union was rehearsing.

"Guess who our new youth conference president is," one said.

"Pastor Thompson gave him a good nomination speech," said the other. "You'll never guess."

About that time my sister Irene saw me. She smiled and asked, "Did they tell you who got elected as conference president?"

Before she could say anything more, someone rushed up and began pumping my hand. "Congratulations, Mr. President!" And suddenly there was a whole crowd of well-wishers.

I was proud to have been elected, but fearful of having to take over center stage. I had always been shy and reserved, except among intimate circles of family and friends. For some reason known only to my mother, I had been christened Carol Jean. That name had been instrumental in keeping me out of the limelight. All through grade school, I was teased, "Carol is a girl's name!"

My name helped me develop into the fastest runner in the whole neighborhood. Mother had a practice of rounding up my brothers and me by standing on our porch and hollering in her strong alto voice, "Orlo, LaVerne, and Carol Jean!" I was always the first to arrive home. I tried desperately to get there before she announced my name to the neighborhood once more.

When I was in high school, one of my classmates learned my full name one day, and he made life miserable for me for a long time. In class and out in the street he never missed an opportunity to announce, "There's Carol Jean Christianson!"

The whole purpose of my enlisting in the Marines instead of waiting to be drafted had been to avoid having my full name printed on the front page of our local newspaper, the Blue Earth *Post*. One of the benefits of being in the Marine Corps was that everyone was called by his last name or an abbreviation of it. From bootcamp onward I was known as Chris Christianson, except on the official records. The only reluctance I experienced when I left the Marines to become a civilian was that I hated to become known as Carol once again.

Soon after I returned home, I visited an attorney and asked him to draw up papers for changing my name. When the lawyer asked, "What have you chosen for your new name?" I was stunned. I had been so eager to rid myself of the old one that I hadn't given much thought to a new name.

"I want to keep the same initials," I blurted.

"Just your initials?" he asked. "That could cause you a lot of problems."

"Okay," I said. "Change my name to Charles James."

"We'll draw your petition up that way," he said, "but if you change your mind, let us know."

That same evening I attended a meeting at our church. I casually mentioned to Pastor Thompson that I was planning to change my name.

"You are?" His voice had the strangest tone. He didn't say another word, but I got the feeling that changing my name would remove it from the Book of Life in Heaven. I spoke to the attorney about this. He was very understanding.

"Tell you what: I'll keep your petition on file," he said. "If you make up your mind to go through with it, we'll proceed." The petition remained in his files for another six years.

Being elected conference president of the Luther League gave me one great lump of anxiety in the pit of my stomach. I was terrified at the thought of having to speak in front of that audience. I ate very little of the tasty food the Elmore Lutheran ladies had prepared for supper, and would sooner have participated in another assault landing with the Marines than have to address the conference that night. Actually, all I had to do was appear on the stage and make a brief announcement, but it loomed as large as a two-hour oration. Silently I practiced my few words over and over, certain that I would have a complete mental block as soon as I was introduced. As it turned out, I performed with a passing grade. Not too high, but passing.

I didn't realize it right away, but before I had served many weeks in my new office, I came to recognize that truly "God moves in mysterious ways His wonders to perform." He was beginning to re-set the spiritual anchors of my life. During the following months, I found the old gnawing thought of the ministry coming back to haunt me. Did God really want me in the ministry—on His own terms, of course?

Soon there was a meeting of all conference presidents of our district at the denominational headquarters in Minneapolis. At this meeting, the national youth director spoke of the dire need for more pastors, and through him God was speaking right to my heart.

The thought of four years of college and then three or four more years of seminary didn't appeal to me. I had never been particularly excited about going to school. I always got passing grades, but I spent very little time studying, only enough to get by.

In the months that followed, the Lord didn't allow me any peace. The old torment returned with renewed insistence. Did God really want me in the ministry, or did He have something else in mind for me? After agonizing over this question for a few days, I would try to ignore it, hoping it would go away. But relentlessly, it would return to the forefront of my thinking.

I had a secure job, and had received several raises in pay during my first eighteen months at the ice cream plant, besides being given a substantial share-of-the-profits bonus every six months. I had planned a financial program for the next ten years, and I was more than a little reluctant to trade my present security for the unknown future of higher education.

Every time I succeeded in putting the ministry out of my conscious thought, the Lord would get me involved in some Luther League rally, youth meeting, or planning session that brought me face-to-face anew with the call to the ministry. But whenever I had to speak before a group, I died a thousand deaths. How could I possibly fulfill my responsibilities as a pastor?

One Sunday evening, I mentioned my dilemma to a lovely girl whom I drove home after a League meeting. We visited for a couple of hours, during which time I related the whole episode of my tormenting indecision. The girl was a patient listener—the prime prerequisite for a counselor. She didn't offer any off-the-top-of-the-head suggestions. Her sincere interest allowed me once more to lay out in sequence the working of God in my life.

A few days later the girl told me she had spoken to her mother about my problem, and that her mother would like to talk with me some time. The next day I invited myself over for coffee. Mrs. Gunderson came right to the point.

"JoAnn tells me you have been thinking about entering the ministry."

"I've had quite a struggle over it," I confessed.

"JoAnn mentioned that to me, and that's why I wanted to talk to you." She offered me a chocolate chip cookie, and then continued speaking. "I believe that when a person feels an urge toward the ministry, that is God's call," she said. "And when a person then keeps thinking of reasons *not* to go into the ministry, that is Satan trying to talk him out of it."

I drained my coffee cup in one long swallow. "That makes

sense to me," I said. I thanked Mrs. Gunderson for her concern and her help. As I took hold of the doorknob to leave, I again experienced a wonderful sense of peace and well-being. I knew beyond all doubt at that moment that God wanted me in the ministry.

Here once more, God had spoken to me through another person. Not once since that moment have I wavered from the conviction that God wanted to use my life, and that He wanted me in the ministry.

That fall I began my pre-seminary studies at St. Olaf College in Northfield, Minnesota. While there, I studied many of the world religions, various philosophies, and became aware of the denominational differences within Christian thought. This raised many questions in my mind, for which I wanted answers. The two questions which bothered me most were: why all the division or denominations in the church, and what is required for one's salvation?

At the close of my junior year at college, I decided to spend the summer searching the Scriptures for some answers. I had read many books that defined the various doctrines held by the different segments of Christianity. But now I felt a deep hunger for getting into the Bible itself, a need to read longer segments of Scripture, not just the usual chapter or two a day.

I wanted to get away from everyone and everything. I took my Bible and my hymnbook, a change of clothes, and my bedroll and hitchhiked out to Glacier Park in Montana. I hiked away from civilization to a quiet mountain in the Montana Rockies. Surrounded by a heavy stand of jack pines, I constructed a crude lean-to of deadfall logs and branches. It was by no means waterproof, but it afforded me a sense of protection. A small stream flowed by my clumsy campsite, providing me with ice cold drinking water and a bone-chilling bath. A few friendly chipmunks and marmots kept me company.

One night a bear mauled through my precious few belongings to retrieve a candy bar I had stashed in a jacket pocket. The next morning, I awoke early to see a deer drinking from the stream just a few feet from me. It reminded me of a scene on a jigsaw puzzle I had daydreamed over when I was ten years old.

In this quiet, lovely, mountain setting I read through the Bible in a week. When I tired of reading, I would sing hymns. I fasted most of that time, too.

What I was searching for was a key that would open the way to a God-pleasing life. I wanted to know some specific answers, as well as what God's word and will for me were. It was a beautiful week, and I felt unusually close to Him, but when I had at last read the Bible through to the final chapter, my spirit was downcast. I had not found any answers. It was with a heavy heart that I came down from my mountain retreat.

I was hungry from fasting, and cooked a small pot of oatmeal at a picnic shelter in a park at West Glacier. The food gave my spirit a boost, and I spent most of that day sitting beside the Flathead River, praying and meditating. Late in the afternoon, I reviewed some of the Bible verses I had singled out during my week of reading, and when I came again to Acts 16:31, I realized that here was the key I had been searching for: "Believe in the Lord Jesus, and you will be saved." That was the answer Paul gave the Philippian jailer when he asked, "What must I do to be saved?"

I had known for many years that Jesus had died for the sins of the world, but there seemed to be so many pious barnacles attached to my Christian faith that I couldn't recognize the real shape of it. At that moment in the late afternoon of that day, something happened to me. I felt a joy and excitement about my faith that I had not known before. My spirit soared with assurance. I was excited and happy. Not only had Jesus died for the sins of the world, but He had died for mine.

At that instant, I knew beyond all doubt that He had taken all the sin and guilt off my shoulders. And right then and there I made a definite decision to accept Jesus Christ into my life as my personal Savior. Simultaneously, Jesus became so real to me that I wanted to share this reality with someone.

There was a girl I knew from college working at the hotel in East Glacier Park, and I hitchhiked the next day to see her. She was a dedicated Christian, and I wanted her to experience the same delight I felt.

Joy took part of the afternoon off, so I could share with her some of the Bible passages that had been so illumined with meaning for me. We found a secluded spot near the golf course where we could see the snowcapped mountain peaks in all their majestic beauty. Only a few fluffy cumulus clouds drifted lazily through the big, blue Montana sky.

We sat near some clumps of bear grass, and I opened my Bible to Acts 16.

"Do you remember the incident about Paul and Silas in Philippi?" I asked.

"Is that where they were followed by the little slave girl who had a spirit of divination?" asked Joy.

"That's it."

"Then Paul and Silas were put in prison," she said, "because Paul cast the demon out of the girl, and that made her owners angry."

"Yes," I went on, "and after the earthquake, Paul and Silas stopped the jailer as he was about to kill himself."

"I remember all that," said Joy patiently. "What's the point?"

"Well, when the jailer asked Paul what he needed to do to be saved, Paul said, 'Believe in the Lord Jesus, and you will be saved.'"

"Of course," she said. "What did you expect him to say?"

Joy had never become entangled with salvation-by-be-good-ism as I had, so she was not familiar with the sudden freedom I had experienced. I shared several other Scripture passages that had become so meaningful to me. I especially appreciated the comparison that Jesus made in John 3:14 with the incident of

Moses being instructed to put a serpent on a pole in Numbers 21:4-9.

"I'm aware of all these passages, Chris," she said. "We covered them in confirmation instruction."

I realized it must have sounded like I had just discovered these passages. The fact is, I had known them well, many of them from memory. Only now, somehow they had really come alive to me, and it was discouraging to find I couldn't make them come equally alive for someone else.

I have since learned that there are different depths to the Scriptures. The Bible can be compared to a pool of water. It looks different from various viewpoints. A person standing at a distance can see only the surface of the water. One looking directly into the water can see its very depths and all it contains. Both are looking at the same pool, but they see different things. One sees the surface beauty, while the other sees the very life within the depths.

So it is with reading the Scripture. It can be read and appreciated on the surface level. There is beauty and simple meaning in the narrative. But the deeper one goes, the more power and life there is.

I came to realize that all denominations who taught and believed Jesus Christ was the Savior were included in His flock. Denominations were encrusted with various religious barnacles, even as I had been, but anyone, regardless of his circumstances or background, who received Jesus as Savior belonged to Him.

I began to see Jesus Christ and the Bible through new eyes. No longer was I concerned with what others said or believed about Christianity, only with what God had to say in His Word.

> To thee, O Lord, I call;
>   my rock, be not deaf to me
> lest, if thou be silent to me,
>   I become like those who go down to the Pit.
>
> *Psalm 28:1*

Chapter *III*

THE SUMMER OF 1951, after I graduated from St. Olaf College, I realized I was twenty-seven and ought to be thinking about settling down. I had always assumed that one day I would get married and raise a family. I was dating a few girls, none of whom seemed interested in me. One morning I awoke very early, and for some reason, began seriously contemplating marriage. I mentally reviewed the eligible girls I knew and determined my chances were quite slim. Finally, I turned the whole matter over to the Lord. "Lord, if You intend me to marry, You had better show me the girl—and the sooner the better."

About an hour later, I was on my way to work when I met a close friend of mine. "You're just the guy I wanted to see," Bob said with a broad smile. "I've got a blind date for you to take on a picnic Friday night." He stood, waiting for the traditional grimace.

Instead, I immediately felt excitement and joy bubbling up within me. I could barely contain my enthusiasm as I replied, "That sounds like a real winner!"

Bob's eyebrows went up, and he went on to explain that he had met Elaine Hellevik at a conference of Lutheran college students, and had asked her for a date. She had an older sister. "Anne's a schoolteacher," Bob said. "But she's a knockout, and she can play the piano, too."

"You don't have to sell her to me," I said, laughing. "I'm ready and willing."

I couldn't blame Bob for being slightly mystified at my reaction; I had had my share of disappointing experiences with dates arranged by family members and friends as being, "just the right girl for you." I was always puzzled why others thought these candidates were just right for me. But I knew without even having seen Anne that this time it was God who had chosen her.

That very day I took steps to officially change my name. I phoned the attorney who had filed away my petition almost six years earlier. "I've decided to change my name to Christopher J.," I said. The attorney said I might as well spell out the middle initial. "That will save you a lot of unnecessary explanation," he said. Two days later on a Thursday morning, the day before my first date with Anne, I appeared before the circuit judge with my petition. He read it quickly, said, "I don't blame you a bit," and signed it.

I chose Christopher for my new name for two reasons. One friend at college assumed that my nickname, Chris, was a contraction. He often called me Christopher, and I liked the sound of it. I also knew from my Greek studies that the name was derived from two Greek words which meant "Christ" and "bearing"—not a bad name for a pastor.

Meanwhile, Bob had written Elaine that he had made arrangements with the fellow who would be Anne's date for Friday evening. "His name is Chris Christianson," he wrote, "and he's freckle-faced, five by five, with fallen arches, false teeth, and a few other minor shortcomings—but actually, he's a real nice guy."

Bob's intended humor was completely lost on the two girls, who took him seriously. Elaine was disgusted, and Anne was angry. Anne decided that before Bob and I arrived, she would go to a girl friend's house, pretending she had completely forgotten about our date.

The girls lived in North Mankato, Minnesota, about forty-five miles from Blue Earth where Bob and I lived. Anne's plan was foiled when Bob and I arrived an hour early, to find her with her hair still in curlers and minus her makeup. She was completely flustered when we were introduced, but I was very pleased to see that she lived up to her advance billing. I grinned at her and wanted to come right out and say, "You don't know it yet, but I'm going to marry you."

The four of us enjoyed a perfect picnic along a lakeshore. I could sense that Anne and I felt a deep attraction for each other, even though our evening's conversation was light and humorous. For a long while after we had eaten, we silently watched the golden moon rise over the shimmering lake. Then we walked slowly back to the car.

Anne and I sat in the back seat, close to each other and holding hands. But there was plenty of room in the front seat between Bob and Elaine. As we drove slowly back to town, Bob found some nice dance music on the radio. Then he suggested, "Let's dance."

When the girls said okay, Bob stopped the car. He opened the trunk lid so we could hear the music through the rear speakers, and we danced several numbers on the asphalt roadway. Whenever a car approached, we all pretended we were having tire trouble. Then, as soon as the car disappeared down the road, we would resume our dancing. We had great fun until eleven o'clock, when it seemed all the radio stations had a half-hour of news. We headed home with Anne and me tightly holding hands, and Bob and Elaine holding a conversation.

We all laughed and joked as Bob and I walked the girls to

their door. It didn't take Bob long to say goodnight. I took a few extra moments to tell Anne, "I've really enjoyed this evening more than anything in a long, long time." I didn't kiss her goodnight, as I had made it a practice at college not to do so on the first date. But I did want her to know I liked her, so I asked, "May I see you again?"

On a later date, Anne confided to me that after our first date she had told Elaine, "I think Chris and I are going to marry." Anne had been praying a prayer like mine that summer—that if God had a mate for her, He would reveal it soon.

Two dates later we spoke of marriage, and two months after that we were engaged.

Elaine had been dating a fellow by the name of Carl Carlson whom she had met in college long before Bob discovered her. Carl had graduated and was now in the process of establishing a business in the Pacific Northwest. The same day I presented Anne with an engagement ring, her sister received a ring in the mail from Carl. The four of us were married the following summer in a double-wedding ceremony, with Bob as my best man.

By this time I had completed my first year at Luther Seminary, St. Paul, Minnesota. Anne had already taught school for two years and was planning to continue teaching until I was ordained.

Anne, however, did not find a teaching position within our living area that fall, but rather held jobs as a clerk and stenographer during the first semester of my middler year. Then she became pregnant. With my interest in tinkering and inventing, I had acquired enough electronic savvy to get part-time work as a television salesman, representing a Minneapolis firm, which had turned over to me all distant, out-of-town prospects, most of them more than fifty miles from the city.

My usual day began at 6:00 A.M. with study. Classes were held from eight until noon, Tuesday through Saturday. On

Mondays I worked all day and long into the night. On the other days I left seminary at noon, seldom taking time for lunch, driving to some distant community to install a TV and antenna. It was rare that I got home before 10:00 P.M., and all too often it was much later.

God was trying to tell me something through this intense pressure, and it was a measure of my enormous stubbornness that while He was shouting at me through these circumstances, I would not hear Him. I was determined that *I* would solve our financial problems, but instead I was really weaving a net for my own feet—a trap for my self-will.

As the semester wore on and the bitter Minnesota winter set in, I caught a serious cold which soon developed into acute bronchitis. Over a period of several weeks, I visited three different doctors—one near the seminary, one in my hometown, and one who was a TV customer one hundred and thirty miles from Minneapolis. Each of the doctors prescribed the same thing: pills to loosen the congestion in my lungs, cough syrup to sooth the tickling in my throat, and plenty of rest. The last item was my only problem. I could seldom find more than four or five hours a night for rest.

My coughing became so serious that I often had to excuse myself from the classroom to keep from disturbing other students. One day my father-in-law told me of a woman in Minneapolis who had a healing ministry. I wasn't very much interested. I had heard various snide remarks made by seminary students and professors about faith healers, and I naturally assumed such people weren't quite kosher in Lutheran tradition.

But my father-in-law persisted. Early one morning he called me before I left for class. "Chris, I'm going to pick you up at noon," he said. "I've got an appointment with Mrs. F—— for both of us."

My father-in-law was a circulation manager for a newspaper, and he drove many hundreds of miles each week. He had recently experienced pain in his prostate. His doctor told him,

"You'll have to quit work for at least three months, and then you'll have to take it easy the rest of your life." My father-in-law was confident that Mrs. F—— could help us both. I didn't share his confidence, and my father-in-law was not pleased when I agreed to go along simply to "see how she operates." I had no faith in faith healers, and I told him so.

God, however, saw a need to broaden my education. I went with my father-in-law to see this kindly woman. She invited me to lie on a couch, and she sat on a chair beside me. Telling me she was merely a channel for God's healing power, for a half hour she rested her hands on my chest and prayed silently. I could feel a strange warmth penetrating my chest. Afterward she told me that I received my healing easily because of my strong faith, which puzzled me because of how I felt about faith healing. But no one can argue with success; I had been healed. When I got up from her couch, there were no remaining symptoms of the cold and bronchial condition I had been suffering with for so long.

My father-in-law was completely healed of his prostate condition, too. He returned the next day to his doctor, who examined him carefully at some length. Eventually he backed away and looked my father-in-law in the eye. "All I can say is that a miracle has taken place since you were in here three days ago."

Back at seminary, I tried to share my healing experience with some of my friends, but without exception they ridiculed it. Some suggested that it was all in my mind, while others surmised that all the medicine I had been taking the past weeks had suddenly taken effect. I began to feel like the man born blind who had been healed by Jesus. In the face of massive unbelief, he finally could confess only, "Whereas I was blind, now I see." I knew I had been healed, and I knew it was God who had healed me.

Even though I had been completely and instantly healed of my bronchitis, I still got only a few hours sleep each night and was so tired I often missed meals, thinking that the time I saved would allow more hours for sleep.

Occasionally, when I was driving home late at night, I found myself so exhausted I had hallucinations. I would be driving along, fighting sleep, when all of a sudden, a house, or a horse, or a herd of pigs would appear in the headlights. I would slam on the brakes, but nothing would be there. It was a frightening experience, and it happened more than once.

I tried many ways to keep awake at the wheel. I tried bending a finger until pain shot through my hand and arm. This sometimes cleared my mind, at least briefly. Often I sang until I became hoarse. Sometimes I rolled the window down and let the biting cold winter wind sting my face until I felt awake.

One time I was so tired I dozed momentarily and then jerked awake to find myself off on the shoulder. I knew I'd cause an accident if I didn't stop and rest awhile. I found a wide shoulder where I could pull off the highway and park, just where the highway started to curve.

I had been sleeping fitfully behind the wheel for a few minutes, when I was startled awake by the loud air-horn of a huge trailer rig rounding the curve. For one terrifying moment I heard the ear-shattering horn and saw the bright lights of the large truck racing toward me. I swung the steering wheel hard to the right just as the big rig roared by and slammed my foot onto the brake, shaking at what a close call it had been. Only then did I realize I had been safely parked well off the highway all the while.

Again and again the Holy Spirit was trying to awaken me to see the disaster of my headstrong way, but I responded so slowly, so dimly. In fact, more often I would only redouble my efforts, pushing myself further and further away from God's light.

One of my brothers-in-law was out of work about that time, and I sometimes hired him to help me. Herb was a handsome, ruddy-faced fellow, very personable and easygoing. Raised on a farm, he was a good worker, always reliable. Herb was always willing to pitch in and do whatever I suggested, and he seemed to enjoy helping me with TV installation work.

By now Anne was experiencing morning sickness all day, every day, and had to quit her job. I was physically exhausted, and mentally I wasn't grasping a thing of my studies. Finally, at the end of the semester, Anne and I decided I should drop out of the seminary for a while. Since Herb had expressed the desire to have a business of his own, I proposed establishing a partnership with him.

We decided to open our own television sales and service store in Rochester, Minnesota, where Herb lived. I knew very little about running a business, and Herb knew a whole lot less, but Herb was interested in establishing a business for himself and I was interested in finishing seminary and becoming a pastor. I owned a truck, some tools and equipment, and a little knowledge. I would help Herb get his business established and teach him what I knew. Hopefully, within a year or two, Herb would be well-enough established to buy out my share of the partnership, and this, we reasoned, should be sufficient to put me through the rest of my ministerial training. When I returned to the seminary, I wanted to be able to spend as much time studying as possible; in fact, I hoped that I wouldn't have to spend any time earning an income.

But that was not exactly the way it worked out. We had to borrow more and more money to keep our partnership venture going, always hoping that business would pick up. We had ten employees, and the overhead was terrific. Herb started out as a salesman, but soon lost interest in selling. Then he worked with the service department, making non-technical service calls and doing minor repair work. He soon tired of that, too, and ended up on an antenna installation crew for awhile. Finally, after a year and a half, Herb lost all interest in the television business.

One day Herb informed me, "I've been offered an opportunity to get into a business all my own." It was a large dinner club on the edge of town. "I think I'll like that kind of work much better than this," he said. "It's all inside."

Though I had sensed it coming for some time, I could still hardly believe my ears. I pointed out to Herb that I had had some experience, years earlier, in that line of business, too. "It's not as easy as you think," I warned. But Herb's mind was made up. He was going into the restaurant business, and that's all there was to it. Then came a startling request that revealed to me how little Herb knew about the financial condition of our partnership.

"I have decided to sell you my share of the business," said Herb. "I'll need at least $2,500 right away."

I was completely speechless for a brief moment while I searched his face for a glimmer of a smile. But I slowly realized by his calm, matter-of-fact expression that he indeed meant what he had said.

"Herb," I said deliberately, and as gently as I could, "your share of this business is $20,000—in red ink."

He crinkled his eyebrows and frowned momentarily. "In that case," he said magnanimously, "just forget about my share. I'll make out somehow."

Herb went into the restaurant business, leaving me the sole heir of the television business. Before I had an opportunity to explain to him the obligations we shared as partners, Herb went to see a doctor about a strange symptom that had been bothering him. Two days later, he stopped by the store. His usually ruddy, friendly face was pale and strained. "I've got cancer," he said. "They're going to operate tomorrow." He tried to sound nonchalant about it all, but I could see his hands trembling as he lit a cigarette.

The cancer was in his lungs, and although the doctors gave him a series of cobalt treatments, Herb died a few months later, at the age of thirty-six. He had taken out insurance to cover the debts of his new business venture, but because of the dire shortage of capital in our television business, we had allowed our partnership insurance to lapse.

I had no choice except to make the best of it. I let all my employees go. Then I moved the business out of the shopping center where we had been, and I worked out of my garage at home.

Most of my creditors were kind and patient with me, but not all. The ironic thing to me was that the large creditors were kind and patient, while the smaller ones were unmerciful. One fellow who had volunteered to co-sign a note with me later asked me for a $250 fee, which is a recognized business practice. "I appreciate your help, and I'll agree to the fee," I told him, "but I can't afford to pay you right now."

The man became impatient after a few weeks and had his wife, who served as his secretary, call my shop once or twice a day. "Mr. H—— wants to know if you can make a payment today," she would say in her most impersonal business tone. Sometimes I replied, "I've got ten dollars for him," but most often I had to reply "I can't spare anything today." After a month or so of these tactics, one day he stopped by my shop. "If you don't pay me the rest of my money by Saturday," he said sternly, "I'm going to start action Monday morning forcing you into involuntary bankruptcy."

"That sounds real smart," I said, fighting the hurt and anger that welled up inside me. "Then you will have to pay off the note you co-signed with me," I said, "or face bankruptcy with me." Mr. H—— had painted himself into a corner and was stunned to silence. "It's entirely up to you," I said. "Do whatever you wish." He didn't bother me anymore.

Another man, moonlighting from a large department store, applied for a job repairing television sets for me, part-time on a percentage basis. I needed his expert help badly. He was to receive 75 percent of the repair charges. This would have been an ideal arrangement, except for one thing: he charged so exorbitantly for his work that often the customers refused to pay. Nonetheless, he still expected me to make all his accounts good. Before long, I found myself with several hundred dollars of these accounts receivable, and each week I slipped farther behind on what the repairman figured he had coming.

One evening, he informed me, "In case you're wondering where those two rental TV sets went, I've got them at home."

I thought he had taken them home with him to do some work on them. "What was wrong with them?"

"Nothing," he said contemptuously. "I'm planning to hold them for security until I collect my money from you."

I winced at the cold, deliberate way he tried to force me into doing his bidding. I watched him as he silently picked up a testing probe to begin work on a TV chassis. I pondered his words and attitude briefly. Then I turned off the machine he was using, and removed the probe from his hand. "Pack up your tools and leave," I said. "I'll pay what I owe you as soon as I can collect it from your customers."

Within a week that repairman started phoning me late in the evening, often midnight or after, asking for his money. "I can't collect your grandiose charges," I said one time. He replied, "Then get an accounts receivable loan at the bank. I want my money."

I told him it was bad enough that I couldn't collect his over-charged accounts receivable; and I wasn't about to be paying interest charges on top of it. But he persisted with his late night phone calls. Often the phone rang, always late at night, and no one would speak when I answered. He once told me, "I'm not going to let you sleep until I get my money."

Late one night he phoned when I was out of town. He told Anne, "Tell your husband I'm hiring a lawyer. If he refuses to pay, I'll have him thrown in jail."

When I returned home later that night, Anne was terribly frightened and in tears when she told me about the threatening call. I tried to calm her. "He can't do that. People don't get thrown into debtors' prison any more." But Anne wasn't at all sure.

"He sounded very authoritative and demanding," she said.

That did it. At 2:00 A.M., I phoned the repairman. He was groggy from sleep when he answered. "I just returned home," I said calmly, "and I found a message here that you phoned. Did you want something?"

"Don't you know what time it is?" he yelled. I told him I had assumed from his late calls that he customarily kept late hours. I asked him to repeat the message he had given to Anne. He was reluctant to do so at first, but finally he got up his courage. "I told her I'm hiring a lawyer to collect my money."

"I think it's a good idea for you to get a lawyer," I said. "And before he proceeds too far," I suggested, "you'd better ask him about the penalty for committing grand larceny."

"What do you mean?" he asked, fully awake now.

I told him that to remove property from one's premises without the consent of the owner constituted grand larceny. "If I were you," I said, "I'd bring those television sets back to my garage the first thing in the morning. Then, we'll talk about settling your account."

In the morning when he returned my rental sets, he had trouble looking me in the eye. I worked out a settlement with him then whereby I agreed to install antennas for the store where he worked. After each job, I turned my work orders over to him, and he collected the money until my account was paid in full.

Not long after that, I left home early one Saturday morning to make several service calls and installations. One of the service calls was to a motel where I had placed some rental TV sets that would play one hour for a quarter. In the past, I had been mystified that although the sets always showed signs of use, there were seldom any quarters in the coin boxes attached to them. This fact had made me miss making two payments to the man who held the mortgage on the sets.

When I entered one of the motel rooms to repair the television set, I discovered once again that there was no money in the coin box. I asked the people who occupied the room, "How have you been operating this TV without quarters?" Not knowing the set was my property, they proudly showed me a simple jumper-cord device the motel manager had provided that allowed them to by-pass my coin box. When I confronted the motel manager, he just told me to take my TVs and get out of his motel if I had any complaints.

He sounded as indignant as I felt, and numbed by the frustration of the situation, not knowing what to say, I just walked out, shaking my head.

Having collected a little money at my other calls that morning, I paid some very pressing bills, keeping back only five dollars to buy a few groceries for Anne, our two children, and myself. I drove home slowly, trying not to succumb to total despair.

When I arrived home, one of my creditors was waiting for me—the one who held the mortgage on the rental TVs.

"Just stopped by to collect some money on my investment," he said. I attempted to explain that I had solved the mystery of the slow return on the investment, but he didn't listen. "I would like some token payment on this," he said, holding up the note I had signed.

"All I have is five dollars," I said, "and I need that to buy groceries for my family."

"I'll take it," he said.

I didn't argue with him. I counted out four ones and a dollar in change, and he scribbled out a receipt. I wanted desperately to say something to him about taking the very food out of my children's mouths, but I knew it would only sound like I wanted to renege on my obligations. Instead, I swallowed a lump in my throat and asked him, "Would you care to stay for supper?"

"I wouldn't want to put you to the bother," he said, and closed the door behind him. Anne breathed a sigh of relief.

"I'm sure glad he didn't stay for supper," she said. "We only have one can of soup and some crackers."

I looked at her sweet, innocent face and said, "That's the very reason I wanted him to eat with us."

I was so depressed, I couldn't stay home. For more than an hour I drove aimlessly around town, and then I stopped by the church where we worshiped. I wanted to pray, but I didn't know what to pray anymore. I sat in a back pew, the stinging hot tears of frustration streaming down my cheeks. Something inside me began to break and I cried out, "O God . . . God . . . God."

It had taken three years for God to get my undivided attention. Oh, I had prayed much during those years, but to no avail. The old Holiness and Pentecostal people used to talk about "praying through" to signify that final surrender that assures the petitioner of the genuine blessing of God. All along, my prayers had demanded of God that He meet *my* condition, but that day I began to surrender to *His* terms—I began to pray through. A strange and yet familiar peace embraced my spirit.

After a long time, I left the church, my spirit buoyant—even though no circumstance had changed. On the way home, I found myself stopping at a diner for a cup of coffee, paying for it with the last change I had in the world. As I sat enjoying the hot, black brew, one of the waitresses came over to me and asked my name. When I told her, she said, "That's what I thought, but I wanted to be sure." Then she retreated into the kitchen and returned with her purse. "I've been wanting to pay you something on my overdue account," she said, handing me ten dollars.

My heart leaped with joy. Oh, God, thank you! I fought to hold back the tears that welled up in my eyes. I thanked the woman and told her she was an answer to prayer. I had just spent my last dime, and now I had ten whole dollars for groceries.

A few days later, the shopping center where my television shop had been located asked me to remove our sign from the roof of the store we had formerly rented. The next morning as I stood atop the store's marquee to begin the task, a car stopped across the street, and a man dressed in a neat business suit got out of the car and walked toward me.

"What are you going to do with that sign?" he shouted.

"I'm taking it down," I said. "Why?" By now the man was standing only a few feet below me.

"Last evening I happened to drive past here and saw your store was empty," he said. "I thought you might be going out of business, and I wondered what you were going to do with that sign."

I didn't know anything to do with it other than haul it to the junk yard, but I didn't tell him that. "Why do you ask?" I said again.

"I own a store by the same name in southern Illinois," he said, "and that's a good-looking sign. I like it. If it's for sale, I want to buy it."

I told him what I had paid for it, he made me a good offer, and in less than a minute I was seventy dollars richer than I had been when I got up on the roof.

My heart bubbled with praise to God for more than the money. For some time I had been asking God whether I should disengage myself from business and return to the seminary, for at no time had I given up the goal of being a pastor. The events of the past few days just had to be His answer.

Chapter IV

HOW MUCH GRIEF and pain I could have spared myself if I had only the sense and humility to apply my wartime lessons in listening to God to my life in the postwar years. If I had but asked Him for His will and direction—but I stubbornly made my own decisions and then had the gall to expect God to bless them.

I felt I was doing the right thing when I discontinued my seminary training to go into business with my brother-in-law. I believed my motives were right. They were unselfish, I thought. I meant well. *But I failed to consult God about what He wanted me to do.*

Nothing, praise God, worked out as I had planned. And after three years in the business world, I finally arrived at a point of desperation where I broke before God in real surrender. And as I did, faith began to breathe in my life again. I actually listened to Him speak to me about re-entering seminary without my usual unbelieving objections that there was no money; instead, I simply trusted Him to supply the means for what He had told me to do. I don't want to give the impression that everything became a breeze, because it didn't, but as soon as I agreed I would return to school, every obstacle melted away. Now God was paving the way for my return to His plan and will for my life. At the beginning of the next term, I was back in Luther Theological Seminary, St. Paul, Minnesota, finishing my second year.

It is customary, after finishing the second year, for seminarians to serve one year of internship in a parish under the guidance of an experienced pastor. I wasn't given an internship assignment because of the burden it would add to my already strained financial position. Instead of internship, I began my senior year. Desperately in need of a part-time job, I hoped for a position in a parish where I could gain some experience, and watched the bulletin board for help-wanted notices. I called each situation as soon as it was posted, but it seemed that the positions were already filled before the notices were posted.

How long it took me to learn! After several frustrating, fruitless days, it dawned on me that God knew exactly what He wanted for me. Late that afternoon in my room at the seminary dorm, I knelt in prayer. I laid everything before the Lord and asked Him His will for me.

While I was still praying, the telephone rang. It was the pastor of a large suburban congregation. "This is Pastor Bingea," he said. "Are you still open for a job?" My heart skipped a beat, and trying to sound as nonchalant as possible, I assured him I was still available.

"I'll drop by the sem to see you tonight at nine," he said. "Don't accept another position until I talk to you."

That evening I was given the duties of liturgist and youth director at House of Prayer Lutheran Church in Richfield, Minnesota, a suburb of Minneapolis. It was a most marvelous opportunity for me. I learned a great deal from Pastor Bingea and gained valuable experience in working with a congregation. Later, in comparing notes with some of my friends who had gone out on internship, I believe I got as much, if not more, practical learning and experience from this position as many of them had received.

It was now 1957. It had taken ten years of my life to complete my ministerial training; four at college, three in business, and three at seminary. During those years when asked where I would like to be called, I always gave a stock answer. Without really knowing why, I invariably replied, "I don't care where I go, as long as it isn't South Dakota."

The Lord was not impressed with my prejudices. He saw to it that my first parish was in South Dakota. God demands obedience, and perfect obedience makes no exception. But perhaps the Lord wanted to impress upon me that that part of His creation which is called South Dakota is also beautiful.

I served a parish of four small country churches, each surrounded by its own cemetery. The churches were only a few miles apart, built when horses were the main means of transportation. The countryside, with small farms occupying the gentle rolling landscape, was much like the area in southern Minnesota where I was raised, except that there were fewer trees in South Dakota.

The first thing the Lord did for me in that parish was to change my thinking about death. Funerals had always bothered me. I had always avoided them whenever I could, but now I would have to face them. It bothered me so much that I asked my predecessor before I accepted the call how many funerals I could expect each year.

He told me that he had averaged four funerals a year. "But you probably won't have any for a long time," he assured me, "since I've already had five funerals this year and it's only May."

I had to officiate at twelve funerals during my first three months in the parish, and there were twenty during my first year. I even gained a bit of a reputation: in our little community, there was also a Catholic priest, and he had an unusual number of weddings during the same time. Since many of the same people attended the funerals and weddings in both parishes, a saying grew up, "Father John marries them, and Pastor Christianson buries them."

All of these funerals forced to the surface the problem I had concerning death. I had seen death in many of its forms, but what really bothered me was a conflicting theology. I had heard and read of death as sleep. One of the favorite sayings of this school of thought is, "Asleep in Jesus."

It was scriptural; people who died were regarded as being asleep. Of King David it is recorded, "Then David slept with his fathers, and was buried in the city of David" (I Kings 2:10). The Jewish belief that death is a sleep is one reason why many graves are located immediately outside the Jerusalem gates along the roadside. Everyone wants to be among the first to be awakened when the Messiah comes.

Our funeral practices go along with this thinking. The corpse is "laid to rest" and made to appear asleep. Yet, as exhausted and tired as many people get, who of them really looks forward to unending years of sleep? It isn't appealing to most people, I'm sure, and it certainly wasn't to me.

Another view of death is that at death the real person, the spirit, leaves the body. The body dies, but the spirit never dies.

There is vast meaning wrapped up in the truth that man was created in the image of God. I have come to believe that at least part of what that term means is that man is a trinity, even as God is a Trinity.

When someone says he saw me somewhere, he saw my body. When I refer to myself, I am not speaking of my body but of the real me which is the spirit that lives within my body. When my mother says that I am just like my father, she is referring to my personality, or soul. In this way, each of us is a trinity of body, spirit, and soul.

God is spirit (John 4:24). Jesus Christ is God become flesh, living in a body (John 1:14). The Holy Spirit emanates from

God the Father and from Jesus Christ (John 15:26). The Holy Spirit is the power of God that dwells with those who desire to live as God wants them to.

At death a person's spirit (the real person) leaves the confines of the body. The funeral is the respectful disposition of the house in which that real person once lived.

When the Sadducees came to Jesus to argue against the resurrection of the dead (Matt. 22:23ff.), Jesus said, "God is not God of the dead, but of the living." He implied that Abraham, Isaac, and Jacob were alive—even though their bodies were buried at Hebron. When Jesus was on the cross, just before He died, He said to the Father, "Into thy hands I commit my spirit" (Luke 23:46).

The Eastern Orthodox Church has two observances for a deceased member of their church. They have a funeral shortly after death to put the body into repose. Then, forty days later, they hold a celebration service to signal the spirit's ascension to be with the Father. The forty-day period is based on the forty days Jesus spent on earth between His resurrection and His ascension.

In preparing funeral messages, I had to wrestle with these two opposing beliefs, and I came fully to accept death as the time the spirit departs the body. This was reinforced by a number of personal experiences in ministering to people on their deathbeds. One was a woman in her mid-forties, who had hovered between life and death for many weeks. On several occasions I stayed through the night at the hospital with her immediate family, expecting that she would die at any moment.

But each time death seemed imminent, she was given intravenous feeding and medication, and soon her natural coloring would return, and she would show marked improvement. Medically speaking, it was impossible for her to recover her health, and the doctor knew from surgery he had performed that she could never lead a normal life again.

Finally she insisted that she didn't want the doctor to keep her alive any longer with medication. She was ready to die, and she wanted to go. I was at her bedside a short while later. I held her hand and offered prayer for her.

She was in good spirits, and I continued to hold her hand as we chatted a while. Then in the midst of our conversation she turned her face to the other side of the bed as though Someone had approached, and she exclaimed joyfully, "Jesus, Jesus! It's You!"

At that moment, the hand I was holding went lifeless, but I was vibrantly aware that she herself was very much alive, walking out of that hospital room into eternity hand in hand with our Savior who has promised, "I will come again and will take you to myself" (John 14:3).

A more recent experience which occurred in my present parish concerned a man in his mid-fifties who was suffering from a rapidly growing brain malignancy. Paul had known for some weeks that his death was imminent. On one of my last visits to his bedside, he volunteered, "I'm not afraid of death. I just wonder if it will hurt—" he paused briefly, "perhaps like a woman giving birth to a child, or something like that."

I told him about Dr. George C. Ritchie, Jr., whose body had been declared dead while his spirit was still very much alive and active. In that nine-minute separation from his body, Dr. Ritchie still exercised his intellect, emotions, and will.*

Paul's eyes were fixed intently on me. He had begun to struggle for breath as we continued to visit. He reached for his oxygen mask and opened the valve of the oxygen tank beside his bed.

"I'd better go," I said, "and let you get some rest."

"I'll soon be getting all the rest I need," Paul reminded me. "Right now, I'd rather visit with you."

* Dr. Ritchie's story appeared in *Guideposts* magazine and is reprinted in the anthology, *God Ventures; True Accounts of God in the Lives of Men* (Waco, Texas: WORD, 1970).

Paul had been an active citizen, and before he had been confined to his bed, he had continued to attend various functions in the community. The critical nature of his illness was widely known, and many people were astonished when they saw him at some function.

"One fellow came up to me at the Chamber dinner a couple of weeks ago," Paul said, chuckling as he reminisced. "I could tell that he was surprised to see me. After hemming and hawing around for a while, the guy finally said, 'I thought you were terminal.'" Paul laughed and added, "I told him, 'Aren't we all?'"

"I don't believe you will feel a thing at death," I told Paul. "In fact, I doubt you will even realize that death has taken place, until you get out of bed feeling great only to see your body is still lying there."

Paul nodded. "I'm beginning to understand something now," he said. Then he told me of a strange experience he had had the previous two nights. "You know I've had difficulty breathing the past few weeks, and the pain has been getting worse each day," he said. "But the past couple of nights, I've slept very soundly. I haven't experienced any pain at all, nor have I had any trouble breathing. But there seems to be another fellow lying right beside me in bed who struggles for his breath all night long, and he moans with pain all night, too. I feel so sorry for him," Paul said, with sincere sympathy in his voice. "But the strange thing is that when I wake up, *I'm* that other guy, struggling for breath and experiencing pain. I think I'm beginning to understand what that's all about!"

I smiled at his excitement. "Sounds like your spirit has already begun the process of separation from your body," I said.

"Yes," said Paul. "I think I'm really going to look forward to this new experience."

Death is a room we shy away from because we do not know much about it. Over the years, I have heard and read many personal testimonies of people who passed briefly through the experience of death from drowning, accident, or shock, and then were brought back to life by artificial respiration or resuscitation. They believe that death is a separation of the spirit from the body. One man who had drowned and had later been brought back to life through artificial respiration said, "When it's my time to die, I want to go by drowning. Everything is so beautiful, so painless, so restful." I told him, "That will probably be the case no matter how you die." At death the spirit becomes unbelievably free and buoyant, without pain and suffering. When the spirit is brought back into the body by resuscitation, the spirit once again takes up the burdens of suffering and pain, the burden of the flesh.

Jesus comforted the dying thief on the cross next to Him: "Today you will be with me in Paradise" (Luke 23:43). And Jesus comforts all His followers: "Let not your hearts be troubled. . . . In my Father's house are many rooms. . . . I will come again and will take you to myself" (John 14:1-3).

Another lesson that was reinforced during my first pastorate, was the importance of tithing. For many years I had believed that tithing was basic Christian stewardship. In my first parish, I had read a newspaper account of an experiment that had proved the power of prayer. This account indicated that where a field and the seed planted in it had been prayed for, the resulting crop had done markedly better than the crop where the field and seed had not been prayed over.

I decided to run my own experiment. I took two aluminum pie tins, filled them with dirt, and planted ten radish seeds in each. I prayed over one tin, its dirt, the ten seeds, and the water, and ignored the other. It wasn't long before the radishes came up, and I noted a remarkable difference: those that had been prayed for were much healthier-looking than the others. Also, there were ten plants in the tin that had been prayed for, and only nine plants in the other. I saw an interesting relationship between the missing radish and the law of tithing.

The Scriptures teach that the tithe belongs to the Lord (Mal. 3:7–12). When a person tithes, he acknowledges his role as a steward, or servant, of God, answerable to Him in all matters. In this relationship, God then adds His blessing to all the steward does. On the other hand, the person who lives only for himself, not recognizing his stewardship to God, and not returning the tithe to the Lord, does not benefit from using God's tithe for himself. God allows the devourer to keep him from receiving full 100 percent benefit of his income. The warning about the devourer is found in other places in the Bible besides Malachi 3; it appears frighteningly clear in Joel 1:4 (ASV): "That which the palmer-worm hath left hath the locust eaten; and that which the locust hath left hath the canker-worm eaten; and that which the canker-worm hath left hath the caterpillar eaten." God allows the devourer to invade in order to encourage man, in his frustration, to turn to God.

It was customary in my South Dakota parish to have what is called the annual stewardship campaign. Each fall the congregations appointed stewardship committees, studied the budget, and made out a proposed budget for the coming year. Then they mailed a series of letters and tracts to every family in the parish. Committee members spoke for a few minutes at the worship services, announcing that on Stewardship Sunday every home would be visited and members would be asked to make a pledge toward the following year's budget. The pastor was expected to load his message with all the stewardship fodder it could hold, as a send-off for the visitation teams.

I took my text on Stewardship Sunday from Malachi three, where God arraigned the people of Israel for robbing Him in their tithes and offerings. They had brought lame and sickly animals for sacrifice, thinking that they would keep the best animals for themselves. Their selfishness was obvious to God.

He said they wouldn't offer these animals to their governor, so why should He be treated so shamefully?

Then God offered to covenant with His people once more. If they would be faithful in bringing the full tithe to Him, He would bless them. He invited them to put Him to the test, and it's the only place in the Bible where God invites people to test Him. "See if I don't pour out a blessing to you," He said in a language that was readily understandable to my farmers. He promised to protect their crops from pests and their vines from being barren.

I deeply believed the truth of what I preached that Sunday, and many families were led to see tithing as God's plan of giving. A number of them pledged a tithe of their increase.

That summer a scant seven inches of rain fell on the farms of the parish—less than the average rainfall of the terrible drought years of the 1930's. Yet the crops looked beautiful. One warm Sunday that summer, my family and I were invited for one of those memorable country-style dinners at a farm home in our parish. Afterward, the farmer told me, "Pastor, I've farmed this land for thirty-seven years, and I've never seen a crop as good as this one."

It was an excellent crop, all through the parish. All the farmers were smiling, and that says something in itself; they know how quickly a few minutes of hail or wind can damage or destroy a whole year's crop. But harvest time arrived without hail or wind, and the harvest was bountiful.

Some of the farmers painted their buildings, and the buildings certainly needed the paint. Some of the farmers bought new cars, and there was no question that many of their old cars were overdue for replacement. Some farmers took vacations, and no one deserved vacations more than those hard-working people.

I waited for the day when the people would "bring the full tithe into the storehouse."

One evening, as I was working in a flower bed in front of the parsonage, a car pulled into our driveway. The driver was one of the farmers who had pledged to tithe. He strolled over to me, his hands in the pockets of his overalls, soiled from the day's work in the field. "Picking a few tares from your flowers, Pastor?" he asked, concentrating on the tops of his workshoes.

I knew this man well, knew of the many years of hard times he had endured with poor crops, accidents, and illness. He was a solid member of the church and long-time member of the council. Happy and confident, he had told me a couple of weeks earlier that the crop he had harvested this year was greater than any three of his best crops put together.

Now he was shy and unsure of himself, chatting interminably about my flowers, my lawn, the weather, and the Eisenhower administration. Finally he hitched up his courage and said, "Pastor, a bunch of us have been talking—" He paused briefly, and then proceeded slowly, weighing each word. "About this matter of tithing. You seem to be the only pastor we've ever had who's mentioned the matter at all. So we've about come to the conclusion that tithing isn't as important as you led us to believe."

I wanted to jump right in and quote Scripture, but I held my peace. He continued, suddenly blurting out, "There's quite a bunch of us who feel we shouldn't have to keep those pledges."

I was heartsick and finally said, "The Bible says it's better not to vow at all than to make a vow to God and not keep it" (Eccles. 5:4–6).

"I know," he said, moving toward his car, in long, rapid strides. "We talked about that, but we felt that we didn't have all the facts when we made those pledges." The door slammed. "Night, Pastor," he called through the open window as he sped away.

These people were reneging on their vows to God, and I was upset because these were my people, the sheep I was responsible for. I didn't know how many felt as this self-appointed

55

spokesman did, but since he had stressed "quite a bunch," it probably meant more than the usual unofficial committee of two or three dissidents.

My thoughts, prior to the following Sunday, were in a constant state of flux. One moment I would imagine myself reading my congregations the riot act of law. The next moment I would find myself pleading with the vow-breakers on behalf of the Gospel. "God gave you mercy, forgiveness, love, peace, and He even gave Himself—because He loves you," I pleaded in the most convincing, shaming tone of voice I could muster in the privacy of my heart. "Can't you—won't you—give Him the tenth that you promised Him?"

The text for the following Sunday was the parable of the prodigal son. I wanted to say, "We have prodigals in our own parish family who now are robbing our Heavenly Father of His tithe in order to spend it on themselves." But I knew such a message would have little merit and quite probably would stir up only resistance. I carefully prepared a message entitled, "The Greatness of God's Love" and typed out every word of it.

Sunday morning I approached the pulpit with fear and trembling. Afraid I might too easily interject my own personal thoughts and feelings, I read the sermon, to avoid getting triggered into saying something I would later regret. If God wanted these people chastened, I wanted to be certain I delivered God's chastening, not my own.

I was relieved as I sat down following the sermon. I experienced a calm and peacefulness that had eluded me since the flower-bed visit earlier in the week. After the hymn I stood beside the pulpit to make a few announcements before the offering was taken. Suddenly I heard myself saying, "Tithing is a two-way testing. People are desirous of putting God to the test in tithing, but they often fail to realize God is also testing their faithfulness."

The words had come out of my mouth without rancor or accusation. Afterward, I hoped the brief message had been understood and that the pledges would be honored. But in succeeding weeks it became apparent that they would not be forthcoming. In subsequent sermons and private visits I spelled out more boldly the clear message of the danger of broken vows, interjecting tones of my personal hurt and defensiveness.

Not everyone reneged on their pledges to tithe; a few grateful farmers happily fulfilled their pledges, praising God for His faithfulness and abundant blessings.

On Stewardship Sunday that fall, there were only a few pledges to tithe, mostly those who had fulfilled their tithe for the year. The following spring we had more rain than the year before. But the rain didn't fall at the right times. The crops didn't mature and ripen properly. One farmer who had a large herd of cattle told his boys one day that they would have to bale whatever hay they could for next winter's feeding. The boys baled the hay on a nine-acre field, and got eleven bales. Normally this would have produced 200 or 300 bales. A few farmers decided they would harvest their grain to at least regain their seed for another year—only to discover that the tractor fuel cost more than the seed they managed to recover.

From time to time during that summer, when a farmer complained to me about his poor crops, I simply asked, "Will a man rob God?"

Almost without exception the farmers would patiently explain to me, "This is the usual pattern for South Dakota. Normally we get an occasional good year and then we have several bad years again." Most of them treated me kindly, but with the condescension that rural people often have for their city-bred cousins.

The Sunday following our stewardship drive the second year, I shared what was on my heart from the pulpits of that parish. "Many of you people put God to the test a year ago when you pledged to tithe," I said, "and He has found *you* wanting."

"God can and will uphold His end of any bargain. His promises are to be trusted, and I have seen this to be true over and over again in my ministry. Those who trust God enough to tithe are blessed in many and wonderful ways, and those who pledge the tithe and fail to honor it experience one problem after another. I invite anyone to inquire of a tither the truth of that statement.

"Jesus reinforced the truth of unselfish giving when He said, 'Give, and it will be given to you; good measure, pressed down, shaken together, running over, will be put into your lap'" (Luke 6:38).

A beautiful example of the truth that God loves a cheerful giver happened in another parish we served, later.

Just before Christmas one year, Bill, a deacon in my Ephrata parish informed me that he and his family had decided to share his annual Christmas bonus with some family less fortunate than they. They wanted me to select the family and give them the monetary gift anonymously. I prayed and picked out a recipient, and Bill's family was happy with my selection. I delivered the gift on Christmas eve, and learned that the entire family had been abed with the flu. The gift was received as a direct ray of hope from their Heavenly Father.

Bill's oldest daughter, Brenda, had worn glasses for many years, and on her last visit to the eye doctor she had been told that she would soon be needing bifocals, a dreadful thought for a high school junior. Having heard that contact lenses often postpone the need for bifocals, Brenda had asked her dad if she could get contacts. Bill had suggested, "If you will save your money and pay half the cost, I'll pay the other half."

Brenda figured she needed at least eighty dollars to pay her half, and by scrimping and saving she had amassed about forty dollars. About this time, our congregation had made an appeal for a special offering on behalf of the starving people of Biafra, Nigeria. Brenda was deeply moved by the pictures and pleas of the hungry children of those war-torn countries.

About two months later, Bill began suffering with frequent severe headaches. Having worn glasses for many years, he decided it was time to have his eyes examined again. Perhaps he needed his glasses changed. Bill made an appointment for Brenda and himself, and then told Brenda, "I know you don't have enough money saved yet, but we will need whatever you have."

Brenda started to cry as she told her father, "I don't have any money at all." She hesitated momentarily, wanting to keep her secret between the Lord and herself. Then she felt she had to tell her dad how she had spent her money.

"I put it all in the offering for the Biafran children," she said.

Bill's eyes filled with tears. "Honey," he said, "your mother and I can only be proud of you for what you did."

Bill decided to go ahead with the appointments, trusting that everything would work out somehow. First, the doctor examined Bill's eyes. A look of bewilderment came over his face, and he rechecked his findings. "Why have you been wearing glasses?" he asked. "There's nothing wrong with your eyes."

The doctor then checked Brenda's eyes. In absolute astonishment he exclaimed, "You don't need bifocals! In fact, you don't need any glasses at all!"

Now, I'm not going to promise anyone that if they tithe or give unselfishly that God will give them perfect eyesight, or anything else. But I will say unequivocally that God will always honor His promise to pour out a rich blessing.

It isn't that God needs our tithe; all silver and gold and the cattle upon a thousand hills are already His. We are merely stewards who are entrusted with the care of God's possessions. The tithe is God's way of teaching us to trust Him and to be faithful stewards. God speaks to us through the tithe, and through His blessing. And the greatest blessing of all is that the tither is made constantly aware of God's role in all that he does, as he faithfully brings his tithes and offerings to the Lord.

Chapter V

IT WAS IN a small prayer closet in my South Dakota parish that I learned to practice daily prayer as a two-way means of communication. My office was upstairs in the parsonage, in a room that once had served as a bedroom. The closet that once had been used for clothes served as a storage room for a few office supplies and empty boxes.

This closet was transformed into a miniature chapel by an alcoholic my wife and I had invited into our home for his rehabilitation. He worked devotedly, using his woodworking skills to construct a lovely altar and kneeling bench. On the altar we placed a large gold cross and a red-globed sanctuary candle that burned continuously night and day. It was a quiet place to pray and meditate.

It was in that prayer closet that I learned to lay a situation before the Lord, and then ask Him for direction. In time I learned to trust the still small voice within that gave me wisdom, knowledge, insights, guidance, warnings—and sometimes even told me whether a parishioner's baby would be a boy or a girl.

I soon learned the importance of beginning each day in

conversation with God. Life seemed to go much more smoothly when I spent an hour or two in the morning with the Author of Life. All too often, however, I made the mistake of thinking I had so many things pressing for my immediate attention that I sometimes went directly to my desk, and neglected to converse with my Lord. Although I fully intended to spend time in the prayer closet later in the day, it seldom worked out. If I didn't spend the beginning of the day in prayer, things—unexpected and often inconsequential things—always managed to crowd out prayer-time.

On those days, confusion reigned. Every task seemed to beckon for attention at once. I may have started planning my Wednesday night Bible study only to have Sunday's sermon preying on my mind. I could set aside the Bible study and research the Sunday sermon text only to have some postponed correspondence plead for my attention.

No matter how I determined to proceed with my varied tasks on such days, I invariably was interrupted by myriad phone calls and unexpected visitors. If indeed I managed to accomplish anything, it was awkward and clumsy. I always seemed to be busiest on those days, but the sum total of my accomplishments was a big fat zero. Even with the number of times I have made the mistake, I still spend all too frequent frustrating days inadequately undergirded with prayer.

On the other hand, I quickly discovered that on the days I ignored the pressing work piled on my desk and spent time conversing with God, everything went much more smoothly. The Lord set my priorities in order so that I accomplished more in less time; I was usually quite satisfied with the things I did, and there were definitely fewer distractions and interruptions.

It was my usual practice, after I had prayed about the various tasks waiting to be tackled during the day, to close my part of the prayer-conversation by saying, "Speak to me, Lord, for your servant is listening." Often the only reply of the Lord would be, "Go in peace, my son. I am with you." I took this as instruction to face boldly whatever the day had to offer, knowing the Lord was true to His promise, "Lo, I am with you always, to the close of the age" (Matt. 28:20).

Other times the Lord would give me a word of knowledge, wisdom, insight, or explicit directions.

I recall one time when a parishioner indicated after a Sunday worship service that he was planning to see me sometime during the week. The man normally was gruff and surly, never satisfied with anything or anyone. He had never been too pleased with me or my ministry, and I assumed that he wanted to make some complaint. It was not without some anxiety that I wondered what he had on his mind. After I had prayed about this matter, the Lord said, "There is nothing to fear. He wishes to ask you for a favor."

Two days later the man told me about a personal family problem. Then he asked, "Pastor, would you do me a favor?" I nodded, and he continued, "I would like you to speak with my brother."

When the due-date was approaching for our third child to be born, I entered my prayer closet one cold, snowy Friday morning in December. I was well aware of Anne's impending trip to the hospital, but I was sure we had a week or so to wait. That morning, as soon as I had said, "Speak Lord, for your servant is listening," the Lord spoke tersely, *Prepare your sermon this morning, for this is the day your wife goes to the hospital.*

I immediately set to work on my sermon, and completed it by noon. Anne hadn't experienced any signals of imminent birth during the morning, and that afternoon she set to work painting scenery for the Sunday school Christmas program. It was the first time that the four congregations of the parish had agreed to a united program instead of four separate ones. Those in charge of this first effort wanted it to be a memorable occasion. It was scheduled to be held in the gymnasium of the public school in town, across the street from our parsonage.

Anne spent the whole afternoon bending and stretching,

lifting and carrying, sketching and painting the large panels of scenery. Yet by evening she had experienced nothing more than the usual aches and pains from strenuous exertion. I was thinking, I wonder if I misunderstood the Lord. I thought He told me today was the day Anne would go to the hospital.

After supper, Anne called, "Chris, come quick!" I hurried into the bedroom where Anne was resting. "The water just broke," she said. "You'd better get Sophie to take care of Jim and Deb." Sophie didn't have a telephone, so I had to go after her. She came immediately, and I drove Anne to the hospital in Watertown, twenty miles away. Judy came into the world at three the next morning. Dawn had arrived before I got home to bed. The Lord had known I would have been too tired to organize a meaningful sermon that Saturday.

The last major concern I prayed about in that little closet in my South Dakota parish was when I sought God's will concerning a letter of call I had received in 1960.

The call was from Holy Trinity Lutheran Congregation in Ephrata, Washington. My wife and I had visited the congregation and community during two of our annual vacations. Anne's sister and brother-in-law, Carl and Elaine Carlson, who had been married with us, years earlier, now made their home in Ephrata, and were members of Holy Trinity.

On our first visit to Ephrata, I had not used my better judgment in a particular matter, and now it returned to haunt me. Toward the end of our two-week stay, Carl had invited me to attend an evening meeting of the service club he belonged to.

At the close of the meeting, Carl asked me, "Want to play some poker?"

I had learned to play poker while I was in the Marine Corps, and occasionally Carl and I had played some friendly games of penny-ante together, just the two of us. We had always enjoyed this pastime, so I agreed to play with him that night.

When we returned to the Carlson's home, however, I was

surprised to see several men from the service club waiting for us. John the mayor, Clyde the sheet-metal man, Dick the fuel distributor, Morry the banker, and Chuck the real estate man were gathered in the kitchen.

This, I discovered, was their regularly scheduled poker night. My conscience told me that I ought not to participate, but I had come to enjoy that game of skill and bluff in the Marines, and I found it frankly exciting.

Just as I started downstairs to the recreation room with the men, Carl whispered confidentially to me, "This game sometimes gets a bit expensive." Carl was aware of my very limited budget, and once again I knew that I shouldn't play poker with these men. Since these men played regularly, it was obvious that they knew much more about the game than I did. "But after all," I reasoned, "no one can lose much money playing penny-ante." I proceeded down the steps to the pine-paneled recreation room where Carl kept a green flannel-covered poker table.

I felt guilty doing so, but I sat down at one of the seven places at the table. About that time, Harry, the chief of police, came down the stairs. "Deal me in, too," he said breathlessly.

John, the mayor, pushed his chair away from the table. "Take my place," he said. "I've got work to do, and I really would just as soon not play tonight."

Why didn't I get up and offer *my* place? What a perfect country-boy that smooth city slickers enjoy "taking to the cleaners." Right then I made up my mind that as soon as I lost my ten dollars worth of chips I would drop out of the game.

This was not penny-ante and I played each hand very cautiously. Unless I held a pair of aces or better, I folded my cards. I waited patiently for good cards and took no unnecessary risks. I was a long time waiting.

The first good hand came nearly an hour into the game. It was not a sure thing, but it was a good risk. I held a four-card heart flush, ace-king high. Dick opened the betting at fifty cents. Morry and Chuck put their money in the pot. Then Harry doubled the bet to a dollar. I decided to play my hand for all I could, and I doubled Harry's bet to two dollars. Everyone dropped out except Dick, Harry, and me. Dick drew one card, indicating he could be holding two pairs or a four-card straight or flush. Harry drew two cards which meant he probably held three of a kind.

I drew one card. I wanted to act calm, appear reserved and professional. I wanted to seem unconcerned about the value of the card I drew. But I couldn't wait and turned it up immediately, like a greenhorn. When I saw it was another heart, I was afraid my eyes would light up in excitement. I barely resisted the urge to shout, "Hallelujah!"

I won the pot with my heart flush.

My second good hand came shortly after. The players seemed to get a particular enjoyment each time I held better cards than Harry, the police chief. There was a good amount of laughing and joking. Dick didn't appear to mind losing these contests, and he evoked a boisterous laugh from the group when he said, "I can see now that it pays to listen to the Gospel and not the law."

"So that's what my problem is," bemoaned Harry.

Although in one sense, I enjoyed the challenge of the game, I was too scared to have any real fun and was only looking forward to when it would be over.

Anne and Elaine were visiting together in the living room upstairs while we were playing. Later, I learned that they could hear everyone laughing and joking except me. They were terribly worried that I was losing what little money I had.

Just before we broke up at midnight, one player chose to deal a game that was not familiar to me. Normally I never stayed in games I didn't fully understand, but since this was the last hand, I decided to stay. The object of this particular hand was to have the lowest possible hand. I had a two-three-four-five-eight hand. I discarded the eight and drew an ace. Dick put a quarter into the pot and threw his cards down saying, "I paired up, but I'll make my usual donation."

Harry said boldly, "I'll raise it to fifty cents." I didn't know what to do. I didn't know if I had a perfect low hand, or if my small straight was actually the highest hand (which, I found out much later, was, in fact, the case). Harry was watching me apprehensively. I decided to bluff it through. When I raised the bet to a dollar, Harry threw his money into the pot and then threw in his hand saying, "I don't know what the preacher's got this time, but I know he must have me beat!"

I was shaking like a leaf as I dragged in that last pot, bringing my winnings for the evening to forty-one dollars. At the close of the game, I felt as guilty as though I had robbed a bank. One of the players said, "It was worth fifty dollars to me just to see someone get the best of Harry."

My brother-in-law tried to console me after the players had left by telling me that any one of the players could have afforded to lose as much as I had won and never miss it. But that wasn't why I felt guilty. I thought to myself, If some of my South Dakota parishioners knew I'd been playing poker they would never come to church again. I was concerned too about the men I had been playing poker with. I wondered, Will this damage their regard for pastors?

The next day a woman in the neighborhood registered her dismay to my sister-in-law. "The very idea of an ordained pastor entering into a poker game!" she had sputtered. I told my brother-in-law that I would never play in a public game again.

The following summer, Anne and I returned to Ephrata during our vacation, and one evening I attended a meeting of my brother-in-law's service club again. During the dinner, I recognized a couple of the poker players from the previous year but they didn't appear to recognize me. The club president looked vaguely familiar, but I couldn't place him for sure.

I had butterflies in my stomach when it came time to introduce the guests and visitors. I was one of the first to be introduced, and was relieved when no mention was made of my visit the previous year. When all the visitors had been introduced, the club president instructed the sergeant at arms to bring someone in from the kitchen. I knew I was in for an unmasking as soon as I recognized the man coming in from the kitchen: it was Harry.

The president announced in a loud voice, "Hey Chief, your poker-playing preacher friend from South Dakota is back again." Then he proceeded to tell about the great poker game of the summer before, stretching the truth here and there, making me appear like the legendary Doc Holiday. It was then I realized that the club president was Dick, the player who had opened the betting on the four hands I had won.

When my brother-in-law Carl had first notified me that I was being considered as pastor of Holy Trinity in Ephrata, I told him to withdraw my name. Finally he prevailed upon me to at least consider the call if I received it.

A few weeks later the Letter of Call arrived. Each morning for a week I prayed about it in my quiet little prayer closet. Each time I sought instructions from the Lord concerning it, I was told through my inner ear, *Don't make up your mind.*

I knew I was prejudiced about this call, but I didn't realize that my prejudice completely blocked God's answer to me.

There were three valid reasons, I felt, why I ought not to accept the call. One reason, of course, was that poker game. A second was that I had relatives in the parish, which can cause real difficulty when they get involved in parish politics. Also, they tend to feel they don't have a pastor, only another relative.

A third reason was that a self-appointed vigilante committee in the Ephrata church had maneuvered the resignation of the previous pastor, who had then left the parish with a nervous breakdown. I felt it would be extremely difficult to come into a situation like that.

I made an appointment to visit my district president, Dr. Gilbertson, to talk over this call. I enumerated the reasons I had for wanting to decline the call. Then I said, "But for some reason, I can't find peace in this matter."

Dr. Gilbertson said, "I agree that it isn't a good practice to pastor where you have relatives as members." I felt a momentary elation. Then he said, "But since they are really your wife's family, this shouldn't cause you any problem."

I still had two good reasons for refusing the call to Holy Trinity.

"I agree with you," said Dr. Gilbertson in his slow, deliberating way that reflected the degree of his dependence upon divine wisdom, "that it is often extremely difficult to minister in a parish where people have taken matters into their own hands, ignoring the congregation's constitutional procedures." Again I felt a momentary elation. But he went on to say, "Usually, Chris, you'll find there are only a very few people involved in such actions. And you must remember that all the members of that congregation, whether they were involved or not, will need someone to minister the Gospel of Jesus Christ to them."

I still had my ace-in-the-hole: the poker game.

Dr. Gilbertson sat in quiet reflection for a long moment. Then he said, "So far as your involvement in that poker game is concerned, I can fully appreciate your feelings. And I can easily understand how you could become involved in the way you have explained."

I began to smile. But my relief soon smashed into smithereens when Dr. Gilbertson said, "However, as I view it, I see no valid reason why you should decline this call."

I returned home burdened with a spirit of defeat. After reporting everything to Anne, I returned to my prayer closet. The Lord told me again through the still, small voice, *Don't make up your mind.*

Finally, one day I prayed, "Lord, if You want me to go to Ephrata, I'll go. Even if it means embarrassment or utter failure because of my previous actions, I am willing to go." I offered myself in complete surrender to the Lord. The decision was entirely His. "I'll do whatever You want me to do," I said. "Speak to me Your will."

Immediately I received the instruction: *Start packing. You're going to Ephrata!*

It was good to have the matter decided, but I still had reservations. I wanted to know how Clyde would react to my decision.

Clyde was an active member of Holy Trinity, and his wife Ruby was a member of the Call Committee. I telephoned him at his sheet-metal shop in Ephrata. He remembered me and our famous game. I said, "I fully wish I had never involved myself in that game, but nonetheless, I would like to know how you would feel if I were to accept the call to Holy Trinity."

Clyde grasped the gravity of my concern. He was silent only a moment. Then he replied, "Personally, I would feel that if I ever needed to talk to a pastor, you would be the kind of man who would understand me."

That reply was the confirmation I needed. "You can tell the Call Committee that I am accepting the Call," I said. "I'll send an official acceptance in the mail."

It was some months later that I remembered that God had spoken to me about this congregation almost three years earlier.

It was on our first visit to Ephrata, the same visit on which I had played poker. One afternoon I had made an appointment to visit the intern pastor at Holy Trinity. The pastor was in Europe at the time.

I was at the church at the appointed time, but the intern had not yet returned from a luncheon meeting. I had walked through the church, and after looking at the attractive sanctuary, I had gone down to the basement area which was used for Sunday school. The basement was unimpressive, to say the least, but as I stood there, I heard the inner voice say, *One day you will be the pastor of this congregation.*

I immediately and completely dismissed the matter from my

mind, not thinking of it again until one day, as pastor, I stood in the church basement on the same spot where I had stood three years earlier. The Lord spoke. *I told you that one day you would be the pastor of this congregation.* And I remembered.

Chapter VI

MY MINISTRY was well received by the people of Holy Trinity in Ephrata, Washington. It was immediately apparent that my reasons for not wanting to be called to this parish were frivolous and unrealistic. Anne's sister's home soon became for me what the Bethany home of Mary, Martha, and Lazarus must have been for Jesus—a cozy retreat where love and tenderness quickly healed the hurts and bruises of the world.

During my first few months in the parish, I received quite a little ribbing about my poker-playing fame of former days. On a few occasions I was invited to join a "friendly game," but it was easy to decline.

During my first two years in Ephrata, the population of the community increased noticeably due to the installation of a missile site nearby. Consequently, increased Sunday school attendance strained our inadequate facilities, and a long-talked-about educational wing was soon built.

Our congregation grew steadily—in numbers. I should have been content, but I was concerned because I felt our members weren't growing in their Christian faith. Somewhere, years ago,

I had read a comment that people would crowd into a church just to see a dog stand on its head in the pulpit; I knew crowds alone didn't signify genuine success.

I wanted the people to grow spiritually, and I knew that my personal spiritual growth was prerequisite to that. My own life needed more evidence of Christ's presence and power.

It was about that time that I read with interest an article that appeared in the Seattle *Post-Intelligencer*. The article told of a forty-year-old Episcopal Church in Ballard, a suburb of Seattle, that until just recently had never been able to meet its annual budget without assistance from the denomination's mission department. Now, since a young priest by the name of Dennis Bennett from California had recently become the rector, things were beginning to happen. Attendance had increased markedly, and for the first time in the congregation's history, it had been able to meet its annual budget without mission subsidy.

I thought this Episcopal priest might have some plan or program I could adapt for use in my Lutheran congregation for I believed that when people's giving increased, it was almost a sure sign they were sending down deeper spiritual roots. As I finished reading the article I prayed, "Lord, somehow I would like to learn what this pastor's program is all about."

It was only a few days later that I received an invitation to attend a Full Gospel Business Men's banquet in a neighboring community. The speaker was this same pastor.

I didn't have the slightest idea what the Full Gospel Business Men's Fellowship was about, but I couldn't attend the banquet because I was involved with an important community responsibility.

The following day a dentist from my congregation hailed me on the street and said, "Too bad you missed the Full Gospel banquet last night."

I was curious to learn about this Episcopal program, so I asked the dentist, "What did that priest have to say about his program?"

A puzzled look came upon the dentist's face. "I don't know what program you mean," he said. "And I'm not sure I understand what it was all about. All I can say is that they have something we don't!"

I wanted to know what that *something* was. That night I prayed, "Lord, I would like to hear that pastor's message. I want to learn what it is that we don't have."

Early the following morning, I was in my office at the church when I heard a gentle knock on the door. It was so soft I thought it must be a shy little youngster, but I opened the door to find the rector of the local Episcopal Church standing there. Under normal circumstances he was not shy, but this day he had a message for me, and he wasn't sure how I might react. "This morning during my devotions," he said in measured tones, "the Lord told me you wanted to hear a tape I have."

As soon as he had said this, I knew he was referring to the message Father Bennett had given at the banquet a couple evenings earlier. "I've been praying for this opportunity," I said.

All shyness and timidity immediately vanished from my visitor's face. "Could you and your wife come to the rectory this evening about eight-thirty or nine?" he asked. "In addition to playing this tape for you, I'd like to tell you about some of the things that are happening in some of our churches." He briefly mentioned that there were some prayer meetings that lasted two or three hours, sometimes even longer.

I couldn't imagine what people could find to pray about for such long periods of time. The Lutheran churches I was acquainted with seldom held prayer meetings at all, let alone meetings of that duration. I certainly don't want to get involved in anything like that, I thought to myself. But I did want to hear Father Bennett's message.

Throughout the day I tried to think of a good excuse I could offer if the rector suggested we start a long prayer meeting. I didn't mind the four of us—the rector and I and our wives—praying together, but for some reason I feared a long, drawn-out session. I knew that I could handle all my prayer requests in a brief time, and ever since seminary prayer sessions I held a keen aversion to listening to other people as they incessantly listed every aunt, uncle, cousin, and distant relative in their prayers. I had finally quit attending the prayer meetings at seminary because of one man who recited the same interminable list of relatives night after night.

So, my emotions were a bit mixed, as Anne and I arrived at the rectory. I was apprehensive as we rang the door bell, but Anne was excited. She was interested not only in getting to hear the message, but also in getting better acquainted with the rector and his wife.

The rector met us at the door and led us downstairs to the basement recreation room where his wife was ironing. The tape machine was set up on a small table, and after exchanging amenities for a few minutes, the rector switched on the machine, and we listened to the tape.

Father Bennett gave his testimony of his Holy Spirit Baptism, but when he said, "The things that happened in the Acts of the Apostles are still happening today!" my heart leaped with joy and excitement. I had always believed these things should be evidenced in the church. I didn't understand what Father Bennett was saying about "speaking in tongues." I didn't know enough about speaking in tongues to even be prejudiced.

While at seminary, I had gone one night to a revival meeting in a former burlesque theater in Minneapolis. During the altar call which followed the meeting, I heard a woman moaning. I thought she might be having an attack of appendicitis, but one of the ushers told me, "She's just speaking in tongues." That was the only experience I had had with speaking in tongues.

The tape took two hours to run, and it was after eleven o'clock when it finished. Long before the tape ended, however, my mind was racing about trying to think of a logical reason why I couldn't get involved in a lengthy prayer meeting at that late hour. I soon discovered, however, that I had been wasting mental energy. The rector made no mention of any prayer meeting. He excused himself to get some refreshments, and returned with a tray containing four small glasses of wine and a bowl of pretzels. He uttered the only prayer of the evening when he set the tray down on the table. He said, "Praise God for wine."

We visited briefly about family and church matters, and at midnight, Anne and I departed for home.

I found myself unusually wide awake. Anne and I chatted excitedly about things we recalled from the tape. We were both happy about the things Father Bennett had said were happening to people in the church today. I told Anne, "I recall when we talked about the book of Acts at seminary. We were told these things were intended only for the early church, to get it started." And until I heard the tape I had no reason to question that statement. Now, I felt a keen excitement within me, my heart jumping around for joy.

I turned to some of the reading matter piled next to my bed, and I read until one-thirty in the morning. Finally, I decided I simply had to get some sleep.

I have strange sleep habits. I invariably awaken for the day at about five o'clock, regardless of what hour I get to bed, and it is almost impossible for me to go back to sleep again once I awaken. I have also noticed that unless I get to sleep by two, I seem to catch my second wind, and am wakeful the rest of the night.

I was still very much awake, alert and excited at one-thirty when I turned out the light. I felt like praying, and so I did. I recall saying, "Lord, anything that will help my ministry, I want." And I expressed no reservations whatever. No sooner had I prayed that petition, than completely strange words came out of my mouth.

My immediate reaction was to rebuke myself for praying

when I was drowsy. But I realized that I wasn't drowsy at all. I continued to pray and the same strange words came forth again. And again.

Though I had never heard anyone speaking distinctly in tongues before, I knew that that was what I was doing. The strange phrase was immediately followed by a phrase in English that I had never previously used in my prayers: "Praise the Lord!"

Excitedly, I leaped out of bed. I wanted to write down the strange phrase so I would remember it in the morning. As if I could forget!

For the rest of the night, I quietly sang the doxology and other hymns of praise and thanksgiving. It seemed I was awake all of the time, but I was actually singing praises to God in my sleep.

No one had prayed for my Baptism in the Holy Spirit, that I knew of. No one had laid hands on me. I had not undergone any personal agonizing. I had simply prayed for anything that would help me to better minister to others, and the Lord baptized me with His Holy Spirit, with the evidence of praying in a new language.

During the next few days, I repeated the strange new words literally hundreds of times. Then one day I discovered that I had a full new language at my disposal with seemingly limitless vocabulary. I could pray in this new language as often and for as long as I wanted.

The first instruction I received through the inner voice after my exciting experience was, *You will heal.* I took this to mean that I would be used as an instrument of healing in God's hand, or possibly that I would have a ministry of healing. I wondered just how the Lord wanted me to proceed with this special ministry. A few days later I shared my testimony with one of the pillars of the congregation. When I finished sharing my experiences with him, he remarked with a note of disgust, "Gad, I hope we don't get that stuff started in *our* church." That remark took the song out of my heart; it also served as a heavy anchor binding me to denominational prejudices and the narrow-mindedness of past generations.

Though, as a result, I became cautious in sharing my testimony, I did notice definite changes in my life. First, I became aware of the reality of God. I had always believed He existed. But now He was near at hand, personal. Jesus Christ seemed to be right with me, a very present reality.

I also found myself reading the Bible with new enthusiasm. No longer was it a book written centuries ago. It seemed fresh and vital, like a letter received in the morning mail. Passages I had only dimly understood, now became pregnant with revealed meaning.

Another thing I became aware of was a deep bond of love between Spirit-baptized Christians of varying denominations. Among them, denominational labels seemed unimportant and superfluous. They did not dwell on the small differences that separate Christians, but openly recognized their unity in Jesus Christ. I also noticed a deeper love and concern for all people, even those who were open unbelievers.

A fourth thing I noticed had to do with my preaching. Up until this time, I could never muster the courage to enter the pulpit with anything less than a full manuscript of the sermon. In fact, I never even wanted to offer a prayer in public unless I had it written down so I could read it.

But now I felt an urgency to preach without any notes at all. It was still me in that pulpit, using my limited vocabulary and making grammatical errors. But when a person offers himself humbly as an instrument to be wielded by the Holy Spirit, and is willing to fall flat on his face, something happens. The sermons may not be literary masterpieces, but God can use them in a wonderful way to communicate with His people and to minister to their needs.

There were times I was convinced the message was inadequate, but invariably a day or two later at least one person and sometimes more would tell me, "Pastor, I want to thank you for your sermon last Sunday. That was exactly what I needed to hear."

I recall one instance when a woman heard something I didn't even say. This woman had been sitting in the last pew during the worship service, right near the door. As I recessed down the aisle, singing the closing hymn of the service, out of the corner of my eye I noticed her get up and leave. She was dabbing at her eyes with her handkerchief. I knew this woman had been unhappy because of problems in her family. I didn't attach any particular significance to this event and dismissed it from my mind. About an hour later, however, the woman phoned me during lunch. "Pastor, I want to apologize," she said. "It was rude of me to leave so abruptly, but what you said this morning about honoring my father and my mother really struck home. I just couldn't stop crying." I hadn't said anything that even remotely dealt with the honoring of parents. "That was exactly what I needed to hear," she went on. "It was just as if God were speaking directly to me through you."

I have become aware of the fact that God deals with each individual in a unique and meaningful way. If a person has a smoking habit that he has tried in vain to quit, and he knows he is powerless to do anything about it, very likely God will meet that individual in the arena of that particular problem, in order to demonstrate His power in that individual's life. Or in the case of a person with a drinking problem, God often will meet that person in the valley of his defeat in order to demonstrate His power.

Some people who are baptized with the Spirit tend to question the authenticity of another person's Holy Spirit Baptism if the person continues to smoke or drink. Smoking, drinking, and any other harmful habit eventually will be dealt with in the orderly process of "temple cleansing" demanded by the presence of the Holy Spirit in one's life, but the cleansing is *not* a prerequisite to receiving the Baptism in the Holy Spirit. I have heard earnest Christians instruct those seeking the Baptism that they won't be able to receive the Baptism of the Holy Spirit until they stop smoking or drinking. This, of course, is nonsense, as ridiculous as it is for someone who is being attacked by a mob of hoodlums to say, "As soon as I beat these thugs off, I'm going to holler for help."

A person being attacked by hoods needs help right then and there. A person who is addicted to nicotine, alcohol, dope, or whatever, doesn't just need help overcoming these enemies, he needs to be rescued from their prison camp. The Holy Spirit is God's power that overcomes our enemies. A person who recognizes his helplessness and turns to God for forgiveness in Jesus Christ, and for the power of the Baptism in the Holy Spirit will not be refused.

God met me at a place of fear and unbelief where I knew beyond all doubt that He made a change. What I had formerly dreaded, now became a joy. One of my members said, "There's a different man in the pulpit now." It didn't happen when I decided to 'improve' my preaching, but when I surrendered to God in recognition of my bondage.

Shortly after I had received the infilling of the Holy Spirit, I had one of those weeks that most pastors experience from time to time and hope they never have to face again. That week my calendar was especially crowded, and I got my sermon out early in the week. It was an expository sermon on the meaning of a Scripture passage. I gave helpful background and included illustrations for better understanding, nothing exceptional or outstanding, but basic and scripturally sound. Undoubtedly, if someone had been asked for an evaluation, he probably would have said, "It was just a sermon."

Knowing that my sermon preparation was out of the way, I plowed into my busy week. My schedule was complicated by a death in one of our church families. This took the better part of two days of my time. Then on Saturday afternoon, an emergency situation kept me up late. Exhausted when I reached home, I went right to bed.

Early Sunday morning, I went to the church to re-familiarize myself with the sermon I had written several days earlier. But now, it seemed absolutely foreign to me. It may have been the hasty writing, or my physical exhaustion, or both, but here I was on a Sunday morning with a sermon that I felt I didn't know. What's more, I couldn't seem to follow the logic that I had used in putting it together. I didn't want to go into the pulpit and just read it; what could be less inspirational than a tired preacher reading a dry sermon!

In frustration I went into the sanctuary and knelt at the altar rail. "Father, I don't know what to do this morning," I prayed. "This sermon seems so dull and dry. I just can't impose this upon the congregation." Very tenderly the Lord told me to lay aside my manuscript and go into the pulpit without sermon or notes. *My angel will attend you, and he will bring to your remembrance whatever you need.*

That was an invitation to walk on the water, as far as I was concerned. I was willing to do it if I could be certain it was what the Lord wanted me to do. I questioned the inner voice that had given me the instruction. "For many years I have listened to this voice; but whose voice is it?" I received the answer, *It is the voice of an angel of God who is always in the presence of the glory of God.*

I went into the pulpit that day, and although the sermon didn't set the world on fire, it was an enlightening message for the congregation—and a thrilling experience for me. It was amazing to me to discover that information I had read, sometimes weeks before, suddenly came into sharp focus on a point in the sermon. Illustrations popped into my mind the moment they were needed.

Many times since then I have had entire sermons come to me, complete with title, introduction, main points, and conclusions.

It's an experience I cannot explain. All I can say is that one moment I have no idea or outline for a sermon, although usually I have been studying a particular text during the week, but I have made no plan for developing this text into a sermon. Then all at once the whole thing is in my mind, complete in every detail.

It isn't always that way; sometimes I have the subject of the sermon hanging heavy on my mind, not knowing how the subject matter is to be developed into a sermon. Then all at once, and usually near the very last minute, it all becomes clear.

I recall vividly one instance when this was the case. In 1962, Veteran's Day, November 11, fell on Sunday. All during the week prior to that Sunday, my mind seemed focused on all the suffering caused by war. I grieved over the agony and suffering that war thrust upon countless people and was haunted by its specter. Sunday's sermon would have to do with the subject of war and suffering, and this was understandable, not only because of Veteran's Day but also because of the threat of war in the air at that time.

President Kennedy had just confronted the Russians about their missile installations in Cuba. Our troops were massing along the Eastern seaboard when the Russians decided to gracefully back away. Disappointment seemed to settle over much of the nation. Many people regretted that we hadn't gone ahead and pressed for a military showdown.

On that Veteran's Day, God was convicting me for sharing that feeling. Over and over that week, scenes of the senseless destruction and suffering of World War II came back fresh to my mind. The memory of suffering weighed heavy as I stepped into the pulpit for the first service that Sunday.

I didn't know what I was to say about suffering, but the thoughts developed as I started speaking. I spoke not only of the suffering on the battlefield, but also the mental anguish of families, and the unspeakable misery of the civilians who often become innocently involved in the conflict. The idea of suffering moved on to the thought that man's sinful nature nurses the militant attitude that leads to suffering and agony.

I am not a pacifist. There are times when honorable people must be prepared to protect their homes and nations from lawless men. Until the time comes when all nations are content to live according to God's laws, I believe men will have to be prepared to use some military measures to keep some semblance of order. I don't like it, but I don't see any other way.

After I finished the sermon and stepped from the pulpit, I felt uneasy. What I had said was true enough, and we all needed to be reminded of these things. But somehow the message didn't seem complete.

Between the two services we have a Sunday school hour. During that time I teach an adult Bible class. I found it difficult to keep my mind on the lesson material that day; my thoughts kept going back to the sermon.

I was still annoyed as the second service began. The message seemed timely enough, but it was somehow without obvious purpose. In our congregation we begin our worship with the singing of a hymn, during which time the choir processes to the choir loft and I kneel before the altar in silent prayer.

Kneeling that day, I prayed in real anguish, "O Father, I don't even know what the point of this sermon is supposed to be." Frustrated and irritated, I pleaded for understanding. Then, in a tone and manner one would expect from a patient, loving father explaining something to his little child, I received the following message through my inner ear: *Tell the people that if they cannot love the peoples of the world for their sakes, then they should learn to love them for My sake, for they too are My people.*

Then the whole meaning and purpose of the sermon burst forth in a sudden bloom of thrilling clarity. It all came into clear focus.

Many times since then I have gone into the pulpit with the general knowledge and information I believe the Lord wants me to impart to His people, only to discover that the real focal point of the message is supplied at the moment it's needed in the pulpit—and not a moment before.

God wants to speak to His people through His Holy Spirit and through His holy angels who are His messengers. They stand ready to minister to all of God's children when we are yielded.

Chapter VII

SHORTLY AFTER I received the infilling of the Holy Spirit, I shared my experience with an elderly pastor who was a member of my Ephrata parish. He was a retired missionary who had served in China, with many wonderful experiences to tell of God's power. After I told him my story of being baptized in the Holy Spirit, he smiled broadly and with a twinkle in his eye, said, "I have been praying for eleven years for this very thing to happen in this congregation."

I didn't know it then, but he had only a few months of his life left. Much of his last weeks were spent in the hospital and abed at home, seriously ill. On numerous visits he pleaded with me, "Don't lose your courage! Don't lose your courage!" He was aware of some of the opposition that was building against my charismatic ministry.

On one occasion when he was hospitalized, he pleaded for the nurses to send for me at 2:00 A.M. one morning. The nurses hadn't wanted to bother me at that hour. They surmised that the pastor thought he wouldn't live until morning, but they were sure he would, so they hadn't called me. As it was, I stopped by his hospital room before seven that morning.

His face was aglow. He was excited, and eager to see me. He had a glimpse beyond the veil of death and he wanted to share it with me. "I've been to the third heaven that Paul talked about," he said. "It was all so real I was surprised and disappointed when I found myself back in this old hospital room again." The good pastor yearned to tell me what he had seen. "But there are no words to describe the wonderful beauty I saw," he said; "there's nothing on this earth to compare with it." He kept interjecting, over and over, two things he wanted me to remember. "Don't lose courage in your ministry," and "You can't imagine how much love God has for all people."

He told me that morning, too, that he wanted me to use II Corinthians 12:1–10 as my text at his funeral. He said, "You can't possibly pack too much meaning into that passage." This is the passage where the Apostle Paul speaks of being caught up into the heaven of heavens where God dwells. Whatever it was that the Apostle had experienced, this beloved pastor had experienced, too.

During the last couple of weeks of the pastor's life, one of his daughters and her family had come to help care for him. A hospital bed had been installed in the home, and members of the family had ministered to the pastor's needs night and day. Often when he tried to speak, he got coughing spells, and his suffering became excruciating.

One day when I stopped by to pay him a visit, his wife met me at the door. She said, "I don't want you to visit Papa anymore. He shouldn't talk, and I don't want you to disturb him." She locked the screen door between us as she spoke.

She and I were not on the best of terms. On other visits I had made to their modest bungalow before the pastor's illness, she had always managed to engage me in senseless legalistic arguments. She would sometimes ask a seemingly innocent question like, "Do you read the local newspaper?" When I said I did, she would come back with a remark, "Don't you realize they carry ads for beer and liquor?" And we were off to another senseless, legalistic argument.

It puzzled me that the elderly pastor had never entered into these discussions. On one of my last visits before his illness, his wife was particularly argumentative. I was getting a bit impatient and thought, "Just this once more, lady, I'm going to try to explain my views to you, and if I don't get through to you this time, I'm going to quit trying."

It had always been my contention that merely doing away with the opportunity to sin does nothing to change people's hearts for the good. When people's hearts were won for Christ, then opportunity for sin lost its attractiveness. With all the careful logic I could muster, I tried to explain as simply as I could why I believed what I did.

The pastor's wife had heard all my arguments many times before, and she showed her impatience as I stated my position once more. She sat primly with her lips tightly pursed. When I finished, she blurted out, "Oh, you're just like my husband. You're both alike!" At this outburst, the elderly pastor gave a loud chuckle, and I felt greatly relieved.

A couple of days after she had barred me from visiting her husband, I received a phone call at my office from her daughter. "Pastor, I've just found out from Mama why you haven't been seeing Papa," she said, breaking into sobs. "Papa loves to have you come," she continued; "he's always happy to see you."

I visited daily after that. But when I entered the sick room, the pastor's wife went out. On most of my visits, I just read Scripture passages and offered prayer. By Pentecost Sunday that year, the pastor was very seriously ill, but he struggled in great pain to tell me he had been awake all night praying that the whole congregation would receive the Holy Spirit Baptism and the Pentecostal power so they could become the witnessing church they ought to be. Once more he pleaded with me, "Don't lose your courage."

The fine old soldier of the Cross died the following Sunday morning during our worship services. I stopped by the home as soon as I could to pay my condolences, but his widow didn't want to talk to me. She seemed to be angry with God because her husband had suffered so terribly during those final weeks, and she was angry with me too, because I represented that God.

With the help of the family we planned the funeral service. For the sermon I used the text the pastor had suggested several weeks earlier. During the message, I mentioned some of the things the pastor had tried to share with me about his vision of heaven. Immediately following the service, the pastor's wife approached me. She was still very hostile toward me. Primly she asked me, "And what else did Papa tell you?"

Reflecting on her remark later, I realized that during the last months of his life, the pastor had shared many spiritual things with me, but never with his wife present. If she was in the room, the pastor spoke of such things as the weather and former fishing experiences, but never of spiritual matters.

In the succeeding months, despite my friend's plea, I began to lose my courage. My preaching was losing its effectiveness, and I soon noticed that I had to work harder to put my sermons together, and it was increasingly more difficult to preach. Eventually, I was back to full manuscripts in the pulpit. This went on for several months. Then came an interesting turn of events.

Almost a year earlier, before the pastor's death, our evangelism committee had made arrangements to have an evangelist from our denominational headquarters hold a week-long series of services in our church. There were several excellent preachers in our denomination's evangelism department, but our committee decided upon one particular man.

I didn't know anything about the man when the arrangements were made. Later, I learned that he, too, had received the infilling of the Holy Spirit, as I had. The way I heard of it was through fellow pastors who told me they had heard this evangelist had "stirred up a great deal of trouble" in another parish in our district. I immediately contacted the pastor of that parish in question. He told me, "A couple of neighboring pastors aroused some dissension because of their opposition to the evangelist's messages about charismatic gifts, particularly healing." He had nothing but praise for the evangelist, and added, "Our congregation is not divided, and there have been many great spiritual blessings as a result of the evangelist's ministry here."

I prayed earnestly about this matter and felt led to go ahead as scheduled. One morning, a few days before the evangelist arrived in our parish, as I was praying, I became aware of a scene taking place in my mind's eye.

It was like seeing a movie on the inside of my closed eyelids. I saw myself riding in a large bus. I was standing next to the driver and looking out the huge windshield. On the highway ahead of us I could see junk and trash scattered everywhere. Slowly, the driver was carefully steering the bus through the debris. I never looked to see who the bus driver was, but just before the picture faded, he said, *Fear not, I will bring you safely through.*

I knew then that we were going to experience some rough going. There were problems ahead of us, and somehow I knew this message related to the evangelism meetings. But with this new experience of seeing a message, coupled with the elderly pastor's oft-repeated reminder, "Don't lose your courage," we went ahead with our plans for Evangelism Week.

The meetings began on Sunday. At the morning services the evangelist declared a twenty-four-hour fast. That evening the church was full. Monday and Tuesday evening services were even better attended. After Tuesday's service, the evangelist and I agreed to have lunch together the next day. Since I had several counseling sessions scheduled for Wednesday morning, he would wait in his hotel room for me.

When I rapped on his hotel room door Wednesday noon, he invited me to come in and sit down. I could see he was disturbed about something. He sat down opposite me and opened his Bible. "This morning as I was praying," he said slowly, "I received a warning that there are some people in your congregation who are trying to ensnare you and me." He wasn't concerned about himself in the least. He was concerned only about me. "Don't worry though," he said confidently, "the Lord said they would catch only themselves." The evangelist explained that the Lord had directed him to Psalm 124, and he read, "Blessed be the Lord, who has not given us as prey to their teeth! We have escaped as a bird from the snare of the fowlers; the snare is broken, and we have escaped!"

That afternoon the evangelist returned to the church with me. Several people were already waiting to see us. We ministered to each one in turn. There were still several people waiting when we noticed the elderly pastor's widow enter through one of the doors. At the very same time, a fellow from another congregation entered through another door. The evangelist knew him as a man who loved to philosophize about religion. The evangelist said, "I'll talk with this fellow in your office. In the meantime, you can continue ministering to these people, and I'll join you as soon as I am free."

I visited with each person in turn and prayed with them for their needs. I took my time, because I didn't want to face the pastor's widow alone. I was sure she had come to argue about something the evangelist had mentioned in his messages. Finally, everyone else had gone. She was the only person left. I could stall no longer.

I went to the pew where she was sitting.

"I don't even know why I am here," she said. I had already heard many other people say much the same thing during those glorious early days of that Evangelism Week. According to

Luther's catechism I knew it was the work of the Holy Spirit "to call, gather, enlighten and sanctify," and I knew He had been working in His strange and wonderful ways with many people that week. What was quite unusual, though, was that this frail and elderly white-haired woman had walked well over a mile and a half in wintry February weather to get to the church.

After a moment, she told me what was on her heart. "When my husband and I were living in China," she said, "I used to beg God incessantly to let us come home to the United States. I didn't like living in China. I was always frightened of the bandits. I promised God that if He would bring us home I would serve Him faithfully the rest of my life."

Now past seventy years of age, this widow explained, "God brought us back, but I failed to keep my part of the bargain." It was evident that the Holy Spirit had gotten hold of her, for there wasn't a vestige of animosity about her. In a very quiet voice she said, "I have come to give my life to Jesus, and I want to dedicate the rest of my life to visiting elderly people, bringing them religious tracts, and having devotions with them."

I invited her to come to the altar rail and kneel in prayer, telling God what she had just said to me. Then I offered a prayer for her, dedicating her to the ministry she had suggested.

As we were still kneeling at the altar rail she said, "I have often heard a voice tell me I should never speak in another language. Why is that?" I had my Bible with me, and the Holy Spirit seemed to take extraordinary control of my being at that moment. I couldn't help marvel at it. I answered her, "It must be the devil," and I flipped the Bible open to Mark 16:17. I read to her, "And these signs will accompany those who believe . . . they will speak in new tongues."

With that she closed her eyes and started praying in a new and beautiful language provided her by the Holy Spirit. It was truly an exciting and blessed moment in my ministry. Later, after she had gone, I related to the evangelist what had taken place. He smiled and said, "The Lord wanted you to handle that one all by yourself."

From then on, I got along famously with the elderly widow. It is amazing how the Holy Spirit breaks down barriers with His gift of God's love. Shortly after that, she decided to move back to the Midwest. Later she wrote, "I never knew the meaning of salvation until after Papa died." I thought back to the times I had enjoyed visiting with her husband, a great man of God, and wondered how often that servant of God must have prayed for this very event to occur in his wife's spiritual life.

Our visiting evangelist's messages had indeed aroused some people within our parish who were afraid that our church was going to become a "holy roller" Pentecostal church. There was nothing in this fine evangelist's messages or manner that would give credence to this fear, but Satan will use any fear to twist and warp reason and truth into a mockery.

I don't believe the Holy Spirit or His manifestations are divisive in themselves, as I have often heard people and pastors charge. The Scriptures teach that the Holy Spirit has come to bring unity among the believers; and the manifestations, be they faith, wisdom, healing, or even tongues, are merely tools which the Holy Spirit gives to be used "in love" for the building up of the Church, which is the Body of Christ. There will always, however, be some divisive people, the "tares among the wheat," within the Church. They are not necessarily unsaved, but they are people who do not display the fruit of the Spirit in their lives, such as love, joy, peace, patience, kindness, etc. (Gal. 5:22–23). Their lives are subject to another force which produces the fruit of the flesh (often very plainly displayed) of immorality, impurity, enmity, strife, jealousy, anger, selfishness, dissension, etc. (Gal. 5:19–21). It seems to be indisputably true that wherever the charismatic manifestations enter a congregation, the demonic powers soon rear their evil heads.

I love the liturgical formal worship. I like the quiet devotional life. And I see no reason for changing any of the solemn beauty or peaceful order I have always been accustomed to in my worship. I don't believe the Holy Spirit is in any way hampered or grieved by the orderliness or formalism of the Lutheran church.

Our Evangelism Week services attracted several Pentecostal people. They were well-behaved for the most part, but a few could not resist their practice of interjecting their "amens" and "hallelujahs." These occasional Pentecostal interjections, even though very subdued, coupled with fears that a few of our people had that we were going to change our church into a "holy roller" congregation, produced a disturbing element within our congregation. A handful of our members became quite vociferous in their opposition. My board members stood faithfully behind my ministry, and several assured me, "If anyone calls a meeting like they did with our last pastor, we're going to declare it constitutionally illegal this time!"

At one point Anne became upset by some of the untruths that were being persistently whispered throughout the parish by those few people, and she was deeply hurt by one member of our congregation. It happened when Anne was in the choir room, removing her robe after one of the evening services. Another woman in the choir stormed into the room, her face livid with anger. She fairly tore off her robe in front of Anne, threw it on a table, and snorted, "I don't like what they're doing to our church!" This disturbed Anne terribly and she hurried into my office where she cried uncontrollably for a long time.

Even the next morning, she broke into sobs when she recalled the incident of the night before. Later in the day as she was putting clothes into the washing machine at home, she heard the still small inner voice distinctly say to her, *This is My church, and I will protect it.* Anne felt much better after that.

That Evangelism Week was a tremendous experience for many. The tears of the penitent wet the altar rail in our church all week. Many people accepted Jesus as Savior, several received definite healings, many others rededicated their lives to the Lord, and a number of people had their interest aroused for the Holy Spirit Baptism. Although a few people had been greatly alarmed for no apparent reason, the congregation as a whole felt richly blessed by that week of special services.

I noticed a few of my fellow Lutheran pastors attending some of the final meetings that week. Only one had remained after a service to watch as the evangelist and I prayed for fifteen or twenty people who had come to the altar that night for prayers. After we had prayed for everyone, that particular pastor commented rather sarcastically, "Well, I didn't see anyone getting healed." Before I could tell of some of the people who had received one blessing or another, he said, "It's morally wrong, if not sinful, to fill people with these false hopes." Then he turned and left.

The next Monday morning I attended a Lutheran pastors' conference at a church in a neighboring community. I had always enjoyed participating in these conferences, the warm and friendly fellowship. But something had changed. I could see three pastors actively engaged in conversation, but as soon as I approached, they couldn't seem to think of anything to talk about. I moved over toward two other pastors, visiting in a corner of the room. All of a sudden they found themselves with nothing to talk about. I began to feel like a leper. It wasn't too hard to surmise that I was the topic of conversation. I was grateful for one pastor who, although he hadn't experienced the Holy Spirit Baptism, wanted anything that God had to offer him. He sought me out and stayed beside me throughout the conference. "I don't understand what this is all about," he said. "But I know what you've experienced is real."

At the close of the conference, two pastors elected themselves as a committee of two to set me straight. One said, "Chris, you're making a mistake that many young pastors make." This remark sounded ludicrous to me since they were both younger than I. "It's not uncommon at all," the one continued, "for a pastor to get tired of following the same routine and ritual week after week." Then the other pastor chimed in, "Everybody goes through a dry period sooner or later in his ministry." Now the first pastor said, "You're just tired of the dull routine of Lutheranism, but by changing that for Pentecostalism you're only jumping out of the frying pan and into the fire."

Now I was not above making immature judgments and I had experienced my share of frustrations in my ministry from time to time, but I certainly knew that I was not trading Lutheranism for anything. Neither of the pastors asked me a single question about my beliefs, opinions, or experiences. And I did not feel led to defend myself. Their parting remark was, "You're just frustrated. Why don't you pray about it?"

I took their chastisement obediently. I may even have begun to doubt in a corner of my mind. How can any earnest pastor help but be frustrated? I struggled to keep the tears from flooding into my eyes.

I could hardly wait to get back to Ephrata. When I finally got back to the church, I hurried into my office. I collapsed into one of the cushioned chairs and cried. Last week I had witnessed cherished friends in the congregation betray my ministry, and this week my close pastor-friends had turned their backs on me. I felt deeply hurt and rejected. Was I really on a wrong tangent? If I truly was doing only as the Lord had directed, why all this hurt in my heart? Why did everyone seem to know the answer without bothering to find out the question? The tears were streaming down my cheeks as I prayed, "Lord, I've only done what I believed was Your will. I thought it was Your direction to have the evangelist here. And now some of my dearest parishioners are upset with me, and some of my fellow pastors have felt it necessary to chastise me."

In the most gentle and comforting tones I was told by the inner voice, *You have been faithful, My son. You have been obedient. Do not worry.*

At that time I was still making it a practice to ask for a word from the Scriptures as a sign to corroborate the message of the inner voice. I asked God, "Show me something in Your Word to confirm what I have heard." Then I closed my eyes, opened my Bible at random, and put my finger down on the page.

When I opened my eyes, I read the verse my finger pointed to:

> Thus says the Lord:
> "Keep your voice from weeping,
>   and your eyes from tears;
> for your work shall be rewarded,
>   says the Lord,
>   and they shall come back from
>   the land of the enemy."
>   (Jeremiah 31:16)

I thanked and praised the Lord for such a comforting verse. Then He spoke to me again. This time He said, *You are My precious child, and I hold you close to My bosom.*

Again I prayed for a corroborating passage in Scripture to verify the message I had heard. With my eyes closed, I let my Bible fall open at random again, and I plunked down my finger. I was using a study Bible at that time that we used in our Sunday school, and to my utter surprise and joy, I found my finger resting on a full-page illustration of "Jesus and the children," showing Jesus holding a child to His bosom.

Chapter VIII

FROM TIME TO TIME during my ministry I have attended various pastoral conferences and institutes where I have heard pastors and theological professors make humorous, and sometimes ridiculing, remarks about people who hear "strange inner voices."

It has been difficult enough for me to try to understand Christian leaders who make such remarks, but it is even more disturbing to me to hear the raucous laughter that such remarks often provoke from a Christian assembly, and especially a gathering of pastors. And yet I'm sure that at least some of those people have earnestly prayed for God's guidance and instruction in many matters.

What a pathetic situation this is! Children of God, the very ones God Himself has chosen to be leaders of His people, earnestly praying for the Heavenly Father's direction and teaching—and then ridiculing the idea that this loving Father speaks to His children. "I speak," says that patient Father, "but you won't listen."

God is a gentleman and doesn't force Himself into anyone's

life uninvited. If someone invites Him into his life, He will come in. Nor is He a "respecter of persons." That means He isn't impressed with people of high human rank.

One Sunday morning several years ago I stood with our Holy Land tour group for a brief informal worship service outside the Church of the Nativity in Bethlehem. There was much confusion going on around us with other tour groups coming and going, and the little Arab and Jewish children hawking their wares among us. I couldn't concentrate on the message the pastor was trying to get across to us. Then all the church bells in the vicinity started ringing, and I couldn't even *hear* the pastor. But into my mind came a wonderful thought, which I know was divine revelation: "God comes into each life like a baby, even as He came in Jesus Christ as a baby."

Jesus was an infant who needed the care and protection of parents until He grew to manhood. God, although He is the Almighty One and the Creator of all, does not come into a person's life with all the pomp and power of His presence. He comes humbly. He comes upon invitation. And even as the Baby Jesus needed to be cared for and nurtured until He grew to maturity, so does the presence of God within each of us need to be cared for and nurtured until we attain the full stature and maturity of Christ in our lives.

The Lord is knocking at each life's door. If anyone opens to Him, He will come in. If anyone invites Him to inspect the various rooms of the house, or the areas of one's life, the Lord will gladly point out whatever housecleaning needs to be done. Always a gentleman, if a person desires to clean house, God offers to get the task done. He does this through His Holy Spirit.

One Saturday afternoon I was taking a leisurely bath. I was ruminating over a text for the next day's sermon on the subject of forgiveness. In a quiet moment I heard:

You remember how you sometimes pray for your children when they are sick? You pray that if there is some way that you can take your child's sickness on yourself in order to spare your child from suffering, you are willing to take it. That's how I feel about the sin sickness of all My children, and I did take their sin sickness upon Me in Jesus Christ to spare them from suffering.

What a beautiful comparison that was for me! I already knew that Jesus took our sin upon Himself, but the tenderness of a loving Father taking His helpless children's sin sickness upon Himself was touching and deeply meaningful.

I have appreciated the instruction and guidance I have received over the years through the still, small inner voice.

One morning, I received a telephone call from a man in a distant community, a member of a sister Lutheran congregation. He said, "Pastor, we have a problem in our church, and several of us are quite concerned about it. Our committee would like an appointment to speak with you." The man's voice was urgent and earnest, but he gave no clue as to what the problem was.

"Sure," I said. "I'll be glad to see you at ten o'clock tomorrow morning."

Early the next morning I talked with the Lord about my appointment. The Lord told me, *They wish to speak to you about their pastor's wife. She is causing much anguish among them.*

When the committee of five concerned church people arrived, the spokesman of the group said, "We've got a serious problem in our church." He hesitated, searching for the right words. "We, ah . . . well—" He came to a halt. Turning to one of the three women in the committee, he said, "You've been involved with this problem from the beginning—why don't you tell the pastor about it?" The woman's face flushed with embarrassment, and she shifted from one foot to the other.

"I already know why you're here," I said. "You have a problem with your pastor's wife." The committee members looked at me dumbstruck. "I prayed about your visit this morning, and the Lord told me why you wanted to see me."

This broke the ice. In candor, but kindly, each of the five told of incidents where their pastor's wife had caused irritation, anguish, and strife within the congregation. "One Sunday she attended our adult class for the first time, and she proceeded to argue with our instructor every time he made a statement. She devastated him," said one. Another told of the women's Bible study. "There used to be fifteen ladies who came every Thursday afternoon—until she started coming. She became so critical of everything that was said that no one wanted to lead the study anymore. Only four or five ladies show up now, and they would just as soon quit."

The spokesman felt more confident now. "We hoped that you might tell us what to do," he said. "This is hurting our pastor's ministry, and if something isn't done soon, it is liable to split our congregation. Many people have already quit coming to church."

Their concern was earnest. There wasn't any indication of vindictiveness, only an abiding concern for the Lord's body, the church. "I don't have any suggestions for you right offhand," I said, "but I'll pray about this matter and will let you know something within a few days."

The committee invited me to join them for lunch. While we ate, they questioned me about some of the things that had been happening in our Monday night prayer group, some remarkable healings and conversions: one elderly woman had had her hearing restored; another who had suffered with back trouble for many years had been instantly healed. One person's malformed arm had become straight and grown to normal length before our very eyes.

After lunch the committee drove me back to the church before returning to their own community. One woman remarked, "That was the best lunch I've had in my life, and I'm not talking about the food!" Another woman said, "It's thrilling to hear that things are happening today just like they did in the Book of Acts." The spokesman of the group said, "Now I know why the Lord sent us to Ephrata with our problem."

The following morning, I laid this problem before the Lord, asking Him, "What should I suggest or advise those people to do?"

The Lord gave me a succinct directive. *Go tell their pastor that he has bitterness in his heart, and give him your testimony.*

I telephoned the committee spokesman and told him what the Lord had advised me to do. "I am planning to see your pastor tomorrow," I said. "Please remember me in your prayers."

The following morning I told their pastor, "When I prayed for you during my devotions yesterday, the Lord indicated to me that you had bitterness in your heart."

The pastor shook his head. "No," he said shaking his head. "You must have heard wrong. I don't have any bitterness in my heart." But in the course of the next half-hour, he mentioned five things that he resented deeply. Resentment is tantamount to bitterness. He resented the fact that his father had worked so hard as a pastor—and for such a meager salary—and had died of a heart attack. He resented the fact that his wife preferred to read and study rather than be a housewife and mother. He resented having to prepare and present statistical reports of his parish to the district and synod. He resented "the social emphasis" in our denominational periodicals and Sunday school materials. And he resented many of the actions of the recently held national convention of our denomination.

It was crystal-clear to me that there was a deep root of bitterness in his heart, though he didn't recognize it as such. With his permission, I spent the next hour and a half telling him what the Lord had done in my life.

It was noon when I finished. His only comment was, "I knew the reason you wanted to talk to me was so you could tell me about your charismatic ministry."

As the pastor shook my hand at the door of his office, he said, "My wife would sure like to visit with you sometime."

I nonchalantly remarked, "The next time I'm by here, I'll try to stop and visit with her."

I arranged for just such a trip a few days later. In prayer that morning I asked the Lord if my timing and itinerary was acceptable to Him. There had been considerable bad weather with snowstorms in that area the last few days, and I trusted the Lord to advise me on road conditions. The Lord told me, *If you still wish to go on to your destination after your visit today, the highway is clear and safe all the way.*

I wondered why He said, *If you still wish to go . . .* but when I questioned Him about the conditional clause attached to the message, He merely repeated the original statement word for word.

I visited with that pastor's wife that day for four solid hours. We didn't even stop for lunch. She was intent upon trying to convince me that "the gifts of the Spirit are divisive" and that "the fruit of the Spirit is the end-product of keeping the Law." She quoted Scripture passages from her beloved dog-eared and dilapidated King James Bible, passages that seemed unrelated to the points she tried to prove. And I read her passages from my Revised Standard Version in an attempt to refute her statements.

It soon became obvious that she felt it was her divinely ordained task to set my theology straight, and I believed that that was exactly what the Lord intended for me to accomplish with her. We both failed utterly.

As our discussion wore on, I began to notice that whenever I countered her argument with what I believed was sound scriptural evidence, her face became stolid and sullen. The moment I finished my statement, she would make a reply that had no earthly connection to what I had just said, and each time she would include an accusation against her husband's ministry. At no time during our four-hour conversation did I say anything remotely connected to her husband or his ministry.

As I became aware of this strange phenomenon I watched her more closely and came to the conclusion that she actually became momentarily stone-deaf to the Scripture passages I read.

She never commented on them. The moment I concluded my rebuttal, she would make a statement such as, "My husband is a good man, but . . ." or "My husband is a good father, but . . ."

I concluded the fruitless discussion by offering a prayer. The pastor's wife also prayed. I remember her praying, "Yes, Lord, I know You were the One who sent Chris here today . . ." Then I continued praying silently for further direction from the Lord and didn't hear any more of her prayer. Abruptly I felt a chill run up my spine, and it seemed to me that the hair on my arms and legs stood straight up. Through the years I have come to recognize that reaction in me as indicative of the presence of evil spirits.

As I drove away from that parsonage, I felt like I hadn't slept for seventy-two hours. I was limp from exhaustion. It was then I realized what the Lord had meant that morning when He had said, *If you still wish to go on to your destination* . . .

I was far too tired and exhausted to drive on further. I would have to make my trip another day. It was hard enough just to get home. When I walked in, Anne exclaimed, "Chris, what happened to you? Your eyes are bloodshot, and your face looks like you've been too near a hot fire!"

I went directly to a mirror and was appalled. I had slept well the night before, but now at mid-afternoon I looked tired and worn-out. My face was flushed, as if it had been sunburned, though it was the middle of January.

I came to the full realization then that I had come under demonic oppression, and it wasn't until later that evening that I succeeded in vanquishing the darkness that was oppressing me.

In his first epistle, the apostle John warns that Christians are to "test the spirits to see whether they are of God" (I John 4:1). There are three ways to test the spirits. First, is the spirit's teaching in accord with the teachings of Scripture? Second, does the teaching glorify Jesus Christ? And third, does the teaching of the spirit witness to our spirit? That is, is the teaching in full agreement or compatible with what we have believed?

A woman once declared that the Holy Spirit had told her, "Don't ever go into a church again." Certainly, this does not square with the tests suggested above.

On another occasion, I was asked to visit a man in the hospital. He was not one of my members, but he sent word he wanted to talk to me. He had been having marital and financial problems and had been distraught and at times irrational. Earlier that week he had made an air trip from Washington to Colorado to Florida and back to Washington again. There were some other stops, too, and it added up to over 6,000 miles of air travel. At first I had thought he had made the trip in line with his work, but when I learned this was not so, I asked, "Why did you make the trip, then, when your budget was already so strained?"

"I just went wherever the Lord directed me," he said.

Though blind obedience is, in certain circumstances, highly commendable, I had to point out, "I don't believe the Lord would want you to charge several hundred dollars for air travel to your credit cards when you are already so financially strapped." The man's conviction wasn't even slightly dampened. He said, "The Lord has been testing me. That's all He's doing. In fact, that's why I'm here in the hospital."

Further conversation revealed that he had been driving on the highway, when he heard a voice say, "Take your hands off the steering wheel." In obedience, he had done just that. His car was a total wreck, and he miraculously sustained only cuts and bruises.

"The Lord wouldn't tell you to do such a stupid thing," I said.

"How else can you explain the fact that I didn't get killed?" he asked.

"The only explanation I have," I told him, "is that perhaps there's truth in the old adage that God watches over children, drunks, and fools." But he would have none of it.

It wasn't until many months later that this man sought me out to tell me, "You were right when you told me God wouldn't tell me to take my hands off the steering wheel. I have come to learn there are other voices."

I had insisted for many years that most every instruction or directive I received through the still, small inner voice must be corroborated with Scripture. That is, after the inner voice spoke, I would pray, "Lord, show me something in Your Word that corroborates what I have just heard." Then turning to my Bible, I would let it fall open at random, and with eyes closed, I would plunge my finger down on the page. More often than not the verse my finger pointed to had words or thoughts that were in agreement with what the inner voice had told me.

But one day, I stopped seeking this kind of proof.

It began when one of my members asked, "Why is it that we can never see the face of Jesus in a vision?" I told him I wasn't aware that such was the case. He said, "I sometimes see the Lord's hands or feet, and sometimes I have seen His form, but someone told me that no one ever sees His face."

I knew of no reason, and I had heard others relate how they had seen His face. About that same time, I read in Psalm 27:8, "Thou hast said, 'Seek ye my face.'" I decided I would try to see the face of Jesus.

For a period of a week or so I set aside an hour each night before I went to bed to "seek the face of Jesus." I read some Scripture, and I spent some time in prayer. Then I meditated. I consciously relaxed and imagined myself in the presence of Jesus. During those periods of meditation, I received many wonderful thoughts and insights. But I didn't see the face of Jesus.

Then one night, after a rather strenuous day, I decided to skip the regular hour I had set aside for prayer and meditation, and went to bed early. I was awakened at the appointed hour by a voice calling my name, *Chris, where are you?* At first I thought someone in the house had called me. But everyone was asleep.

Then I remembered I had made a prayer-agreement to spend that particular hour each night seeking to behold Christ's face.

The following week I had to attend a Bethel Series Bible Study Clinic in Madison, Wisconsin. Late one evening a pastor came to my room to visit me. This pastor desired healing, and he wanted me to pray for him. I did so with the laying on of hands.

Then I asked if he, in turn, would offer a prayer for me. I had no special prayer request; I just wanted him to pray for me. He placed his hands on my head and remained silent for a few moments. Then he said, "I have a message for you from the Lord: 'I see you when you seek My face.'"

I had said nothing to this pastor about my efforts to see the face of Jesus. And the Lord used this unique and wonderful way to encourage me in my quest. He spoke to me through a man I had not known previously, at a point 1,800 miles from my home.

I continued my quest until one day I did finally see directly into the face of Jesus as I prayed. I cannot describe Him, except to say that the compassion and tenderness in His eyes is infinite and unforgettable.

That day the inner voice told me, *You have listened to My voice for many years, and you know My voice by now. I no longer want you to verify My messages to you in that fashion.*

How wonderful that the Lord can speak to us directly, and without our doubting Him.

Several years ago, I was confronted by some Spirit-baptized Christians who thought all Spirit-baptized Christians from all denominations should unite and become, as they said, "the church Christ intended." Their belief was that the denominations were dead, and that their deadness was proof enough that the Lord didn't approve of them. They argued that in a church where all the members were Spirit-filled, there would be perfect freedom.

When first I was confronted with this movement, I prayed at length about it. I earnestly wanted to know if the Lord would have me leave the organized church and join others in some new design for His Church. I didn't want to leave, but I was willing to do whatever the Lord wanted of me. The Lord's answer was not long in coming.

Even as I prayed with my eyes closed, I saw in my mind's eye a huge elephant. She was lying down, sick. I saw people busily ministering to her, and occasionally the elephant would move her trunk, or lift a heavy leg, or twitch her ear or tail. But nothing they did succeeded in getting the elephant to her feet. The elephant remained on her side, sick.

Then came the inner voice with the meaning of what I had seen. *People have all kinds of programs and schemes to put life into My Church, but they only manage to get a token response. It will not be by man's programs nor by man's schemes, for as it is written, "Not by [man's] might, nor by [man's] power, but by my Spirit, says the Lord of Hosts"* (Zech. 4:6).

Man cannot revive the Church by schemes and programs, no matter how well they are planned and carried out. The church will be revived only when God is permitted to breathe into her nostrils the breath of life, His Holy Spirit, which He promised to give His Church.

The desire on the part of some Spirit-baptized Christians to separate themselves from the "dead denominational church" appears to be a perennial problem.

On one occasion, a few of my own members were earnestly caught up in this separatist movement. They believed the Holy Spirit was directing them to leave our church. Again I prayed about this, and again the Lord's answer was prompt in coming.

In my mind's eye, I saw a crockery bowl half-filled with bread dough. It just sat there. Nothing was happening. Then my attention was directed to a dish of yeast sitting nearby. Nothing was happening there either. It just sat there. After a period of waiting, the yeast was added to the dough, and soon the dough began to rise. It continued rising until the bowl was bulging with active bread dough.

The meaning quickly followed through the inner voice. *The crock of dough is My Church. My Spirit-baptized children are like the yeast in the dish. I need them in My Church to put life into My people. It is for this very purpose that I have raised them up.*

It is not without heartaches and headaches that one works among believers who oppose the manifestations of the Holy Spirit. But the Lord didn't call us to a quiet secluded club life. He called us into the arena of the world's sickness, sin, and strife to witness and to work, and to die in the doing, if necessary.

There have been times in my ministry when I would have preferred a safe sanctuary, away from the tension and strife of the battle in the spiritual realm. But I know that if anything is ever to be accomplished in the spiritual realm, there will always be tension and struggle. We are engaged in spiritual combat, even as Paul declares (see Eph. 6).

It is for that very reason that Jesus did not leave us comfortless, but sent the Holy Spirit to give us guidance and instruction. Each denomination has its old wineskins of doctrine and practice. I once saw a banner hanging in a church containing the message: "The seven last words of the Church— We Never Did It Like This Before." I'm afraid that banner would bring knowing smiles in almost any congregation.

Several years ago, I received an instruction from the Lord that was exceptionally meaningful to me in my struggle with new dimensions of God's truth. I had been sleeping soundly for two or three hours when I was awakened abruptly. I wasn't aware of having heard my name called or any noise. But I found myself suddenly wide awake and sitting up in bed. Then I heard a distinct, audible voice:

"This is a parable. A farmer had one goose. And in the spring of the year when all the chickens on the farm were setting on eggs and hatching them, the goose became jealous. She wanted to do the same thing. So the farmer took some smooth stones, painted them white, and placed them under the goose. Whenever anyone came near her nest, the goose would hiss and snap at them."

There was a brief pause, and then the voice continued. "The meaning of the parable is this: When you hear someone teaching in a way that differs from what you believe, and you find yourself hissing and snapping at them, be sure that what you are protecting is the truth and not merely stones that are painted to resemble the truth."

This parable has served as a prod to allow the Holy Spirit to enlarge my understanding in many areas of spiritual knowledge. Not least of these is in the area of healing.

Healing appears to be one of the natural patterns into which Spirit-baptized Christians develop. Soon after a person has experienced the infilling, there is often a renewed interest in what is known as "faith healing."

For many years my mind has been drawn to Psalm 103:2-3 which says, "Bless the Lord . . . who heals all your diseases," and Isaiah 53:5 which says, "But he was wounded for our transgressions . . . and with his stripes we are healed." In the New Testament, Matthew 8:16 speaks of Jesus in the home of Peter casting out evil spirits from people, and healing their sicknesses. Then he adds, "This was to fulfil what was spoken by the prophet Isaiah, 'He took our infirmities and bore our diseases' " (v.17).

It is clear in Scripture that Jesus not only took upon Himself our sin sickness, but also our diseases and ailments as well. I'm just beginning to see that Satan is the one who robs us of health and keeps us from enjoying the blessings God has already given us through Jesus Christ. Many of us learn to contend with Satan over our salvation until we have peace of mind. We *know* Jesus died for our sin and that God has forgiven us. When our conscience seems to continue convicting us of sins that were long ago forgiven, we eventually sense that Satan is behind the scenes. There can be no doubt about it.

Some time ago I awoke one morning, remembering clearly an incident that had occurred years earlier. It was a matter concerning what one would call an honest mistake, and yet I had been deeply grieved over my part in the incident. I was sure I had asked for and had received God's forgiveness, but now the incident returned to my mind with such clarity and vividness that I felt sure the Lord was trying to tell me something about it. I prayed, "Lord, this all happened so long ago, and I was certain I had received Your forgiveness. Why, now, do You remind me once again of this event?" Very gently and lovingly, the inner voice spoke, *I am not the one who is reminding you.*

Unfortunately, God all too often gets blamed for things that Satan does. Satan doesn't want us to enjoy fellowship with God, and he uses every method he can to keep us unbalanced and unhappy in our spiritual lives. When we recognize Satan's handiwork, we contend against him. We state our belief in God's promises, and we command Satan to leave us alone. Then we begin to experience the peace which passes all understanding.

Just as Satan attempts to keep us from enjoying our state of grace over our sins, so he prevents us from enjoying our state of grace over our diseases and infirmities. We must learn to claim our inheritance and protect it from Satan's wiles.

For many years I experienced headaches that sometimes lasted for days. I took aspirin tablets several times a day, four or five at a time, often consuming thirty or forty tablets a day. I tried every headache pill on the market, but none of them gave me any real measure of relief. Often my ears would ring from taking too much medication.

Early one morning I awoke suddenly from a dream. In the dream there had been four or five train coaches rolling down the track without an engine, and I was in one of the coaches. Further up the line, separated from our coaches, was a train engine and some more train cars. Somehow I knew our segment of train was supposed to coast along until it hooked up to the segment of train with the engine, and then we would continue on, joined together. As our coaches were rolling along, I put four aspirins in my hand (in the dream). I tossed the aspirins into my mouth and immediately our coaches slowed down noticeably, so much so that I knew they would stop before we hooked up to the train ahead. Quickly, I spit the aspirins out into my hand again, and the coaches resumed their speed. It was at that moment that I awoke.

When I have dreams that are very vivid, I have learned that there is often a special meaning to them. I prayed for an interpretation of this dream and received the following warning:

You are consuming a dangerous amount of aspirin, and if you don't stop it, you will not connect up with the real purpose of your life, nor will you fulfill My plan for you.

I cut down my intake of aspirin, and for a period of several days, I didn't consume any. As time went on, however, I found reason to take an ever-increasing amount of aspirin again. If it wasn't my head aching, it was a bothersome tooth, or an aching muscle. Often it was some elusive pain which I tried to pacify with aspirin.

Then one day I was again concerned with the excessive number of aspirin tablets I consumed on an average day. I was determined to get rid of my headaches once and for all. I asserted my belief that Jesus died not only for my sin, but also for my sicknesses, and I demanded that Satan let me enjoy what God had already given me. I stopped taking aspirin and other pain pills. After that, whenever I felt an ache or pain, I commanded it away in Jesus' name. I now enjoy living without those nagging headaches that had harassed me almost every day of my ministry up until that time.

A marvelous thing the Lord has been doing in recent years is the growing out of limbs. I had had an ailing back for many years until a guest pastor after speaking at a prayer breakfast in our church one day, pointed to me and said, "Why don't you come up here and let the Lord straighten you out?" I had been sitting at the opposite end of the table from the speaker. I went forward and sat down in a chair the speaker had placed there for people who desired healing. I had not said anything to this pastor, nor to anyone else for that matter, concerning my back problem. He seemed to know exactly what my problem was even before he called me forward.

The pastor knelt down in front of me and lifted my feet in his hands. After measuring my legs, he announced, "Your left leg is three-quarters of an inch shorter than your right." I could see the difference myself. Then he gave a simple command to my left leg saying, "In Jesus' name, grow!" Immediately my left leg grew. I could see it grow, and I could feel a strange sensation within my leg. "Now your left leg has grown a quarter-inch beyond your right one," said the pastor calmly. "This often happens." Then he quietly commanded the right leg, "In Jesus' name, grow even!" Then I saw and felt my right leg grow until both legs were of identical length. I have not had any trouble with my back since that day.

I have witnessed this miracle many times since then. I have seen several people do as that pastor did, and I have done the same for many others. After seeing many dozens of legs grow out, I began to wonder why there were so many people with legs whose length didn't match. I found an item in a medical journal which stated that two of every five people in the United States had legs of differing length. The ratio is seven out of eight in Britain, I believe.

I began to wonder why so many people had legs of differing length. One day I prayed to the Lord about this. He explained the problem this way:

This is a crooked and perverse generation where most of My children know My will, and they know they should walk in My way. Still they enjoy walking in worldly ways, too. So they hobble along in life with one foot on the sidewalk of My will and the other foot in the gutter of the world. Their crooked walk is a physical manifestation of a spiritual ailment.

This explanation reminded me of what the prophet Elijah had told the people of Israel at Mount Carmel, "How long will you go limping with two different opinions? If the Lord is God, follow him; but if Baal, then follow him" (I Kings 18:21). God's people seem to have limped along in every generation, when He has meant for them to walk straight and strong.

Chapter IX

THE STUBBORN, selfish human will has a difficult time getting used to the idea of letting God call the signals. Often I find myself pushing ahead toward a burdensome schedule, wondering how I'll ever get everything done that needs doing. Only then will I remember to lay it all before the Lord, seeking His direction. Are all these things necessary? Does He want me to do this or that? What does He want me to write in this letter to a troubled person? What does He want me to say to this person who is to see me for counseling this morning? What text should I use for a funeral tomorrow, and what message should I bring?

When I lay out all these questions, and surrender my will to the doing of God's will, it is utterly amazing how quickly the pressure lets up. There's a serene confidence that envelops me when I move through the busy responsibilities, wanting only to do God's bidding.

There are times when a thing seems right and good, but I don't know if it is the Lord's will. At such times I ask for a special sign from God to put His stamp of approval on it.

Several years ago, I was invited to a conference of Spirit-baptized people in the Bay Area of California. Another clergyman from our city had urged me to go along with him. I wanted very much to learn more of the things of the Spirit, but it was a busy time of the year for me.

Early one morning I prayed for God's will in the matter. Did He really want me to go? Through the still, small voice I was informed that I should go. Yet I wasn't sure if I actually heard the inner voice of the Lord, or if I was listening to my own willful imagination. I asked God to give me a sign. The inner voice instructed me, *Your sign will be a pink slip of paper on your desk.* I understood this instruction to mean that if I found a pink slip of paper on my desk, that would mean God's approval for this trip.

I hadn't gone to my office at the church yet that morning when I prayed, but I was sure that such a sign couldn't possibly appear. The day before, I had cleared everything off my desk (an extremely rare occasion). I knew there was nothing on my desk, and no one had access to my office. I was sure there couldn't possibly be a pink slip of paper there. I wanted God to give me another sign, one that had some possibility of fulfillment, but I was told that the pink slip of paper would be there.

Later, when I arrived at my office, I was surprised to see on the top of my desk a pink slip of paper. I remembered then how the paper had gotten there. As I was about to leave my office the previous afternoon, I had decided to take a certain book home. When I removed that book from the shelf I noticed a slip of paper that had been used previously as a marker, sticking out of the book. I had removed the pink marker then and had left it on my desk.

Happily, I went ahead with plans for the trip. All arrangements went smoothly. I didn't give another thought to God's will in this matter until we were in flight on the first leg of our journey. Then a thought came into my mind to plague me.

Perhaps my subconscious mind had remembered that pink slip of paper on my desk, I reasoned, and since I wanted to make this trip, my conscious mind simply provided me with this sign.

Bothered with this possibility, I prayed that God would show me another sign. At that moment we were in the landing pattern of Portland International Airport, and I prayed God to give me another confirmation of His will on this trip. I didn't receive an instruction through the inner voice, but God assured me in a different way.

My clergy friend and I were traveling on special passes that permitted a reduced fare, but didn't guarantee us a reservation. We had been assured by our local airline representative that we shouldn't have any trouble. "There are always plenty of seats available during midweek," he had assured us.

We were scheduled to change flights at Portland, and our incoming flight was a few minutes late. Our next flight was already loading when we landed. My friend and I hurried to the departure gate, and we arrived just as the last few members of a college football team were going aboard. The team took all but two seats of the small fan-jet, and my friend and I got those two seats. I was delighted to accept this "coincidence" as a confirmation of God's approval for my trip.

My friend and I spent three pleasant days listening to testimonies and lectures on the moving of the Holy Spirit. I received helpful information and encouragement from listening to the experiences of others. My friend had decided to stay in California for a few more days, but I was planning to return home on Saturday in order to perform my Sunday duties. He wished me well when we parted company Friday evening and said, "Here's hoping you don't get fogged in tomorrow so you can't get home in time for Sunday."

That was all I needed to hinder my sleep that night. Eagerly and apprehensively I awaited the Saturday dawn to see what kind of weather we had. It was clear and bright.

In my devotions that morning, I had felt constrained to

confess my lack of faith, since I had worried about the weather. The Lord doesn't leave any loose ends in His planning, and His timing is perfect. Since He had given His approval of my trip, I certainly should have trusted Him to get me back home in time to fulfill my Sunday responsibilities. When I finished praying, I listened quietly for the Lord's instruction. He said, *I'm going to show you something special today.*

I felt eager anticipation as I rode the limousine bus to the airport. My flight was on time, the take-off was smooth, and the flight was pleasant. I was just finishing my airborne breakfast when the stewardess announced over the intercom, "Our captain reports that we will not be making our scheduled stop at Medford, Oregon, due to fog."

I couldn't imagine how an inland city could be engulfed in fog when we had had bright, clear weather all around us. But a few minutes later we could see the city was socked in solid. It looked like a huge mound of whipped cream scooped up over the city.

Our plane dipped one wing and slowly circled the fogbound city. Then the captain cut the power and we started to descend. The stewardess awkwardly announced, "I guess our captain has changed his mind. It looks like we're stopping at Medford after all." Ever so slowly the captain lowered the plane into the whipped cream. I was particularly alert because of what the Lord had said that morning. He was going to show me something special that day, and I didn't want to miss it.

I was sitting just behind the wing where I could see the left landing gear. I could barely make out the wheel in the heavy fog. We kept slowly, ever so slowly, descending. Wondering how the pilot could know where the landing strip was, I kept my eye on the barely visible tire. Then I received a mental nudge from the Holy Spirit to *Watch now!*

Just at that moment, the plane broke through the fog, and a moment later, the wheel I had been watching all this time touched down on the runway. The heat of the sun had caused the fog to lift a short way, and there was perhaps fifty or a hundred feet of clear visibility between the layer of fog and the runway. As our plane turned toward the passenger concourse, the inner voice spoke: *Even as another person has guided the pilot through the fog to a safe landing, so will I guide you safely through your life.*

In the foregoing incident, I learned that God can and does give assurances of His will in a matter. He speaks to us through signs. I have also learned that we can lay a "fleece" out in order to learn God's will in a matter. This term comes from Judges, chapter six, where Gideon was searching for God's will. As a sign, he placed a fleece of wool on the threshing floor. First, he set the condition for the sign that the fleece be wet with dew but all the ground around it must be dry. When that test was met, Gideon reversed the condition the following night, and the fleece remained dry while the ground was wet with dew.

Putting out a fleece is a good way to learn the Lord's will, or a good way of getting His confirmation on a decision you are trying to make.

A few summers ago I had wanted to attend a charismatic clinic in Anaheim, California, and I had made reservations to attend. The week before the clinic was to be held, I thought it might be best if I canceled my reservations and stayed home. I had a bad cold, and a very crowded schedule. Then it occurred to me—I'm ashamed to admit it—that I hadn't sought the Lord's will concerning this trip. The inner voice gave full approval for my going, but to be absolutely certain, I decided to put out a fleece for confirmation.

By now, I really wanted to get out of attending this charismatic clinic. I planned to "stack the cards" against the Lord by asking for a fleece that I thought was near impossible.

At the time I was praying about this matter, I was driving in a college town, a few blocks from an apartment house where I had to make a call. I had been warned ahead of time that I should plan to park in the rear of the apartments as the students' cars always filled both sides of the street for many blocks during class time.

Three blocks from the apartment, I said, "Lord, if You want me to go to this clinic, You provide a parking place for me in front of the apartment."

As usual, the cars were parked bumper to bumper for blocks along the street where I was driving, and the apartment house was several blocks closer to the college. But as I neared the apartment house, I saw one parking space open—directly in front of the apartment. Once more I had lost to the Lord's wondrous ways. I wasn't content, however, to let the contest stop there. I put another fleece before the Lord: "If You really want me to go to that clinic, You will have to line up the money. I don't have it."

Shortly after I returned home from my out-of-town trip, I was greeted by one of my members, Dr. Jacobson, the dentist who had heard Dennis Bennett's talk years earlier. "Pastor, I've decided to go with you to Anaheim," he said, "and I want to pick up your tab."

Almost any way a person chooses to seek the Lord's confirmation appears to be acceptable. He wants to communicate with His children, but they have to make some channel of communication available to Him.

Truly, God did not ordain silence between Himself and the crown of His creation, man. A person who is open to God's communication will be instructed in divine matters. Moses learned in this way. "Out of heaven he made thee to hear his voice, that he might instruct thee" (Deut. 4:36 KJV). Before Paul became an apostle, he also learned in this fashion. "For I would have you know, brethren, that the gospel which was preached by me is not man's gospel. For I did not receive it from man, nor was I taught it, but it came through a revelation of Jesus Christ" (Gal. 1:11-12).

Many could argue, "Yes, but I am not a Moses or a Paul." I could say the same for myself, and yet God has communicated with me. And I firmly believe He wants to communicate with all believers.

There was a plaintive note when the Lord instructed me to write of my experiences: *I want to speak to My children.* This isn't a new revelation from God. Way back in Old Testament times, God was concerned that people didn't listen to Him. God spoke to the people of Judah through the prophet Jeremiah: "But you did not incline your ear or listen to me. . . . I have spoken to them and they have not listened" (Jer. 35:15, 17).

It might be well to remember that we would have no Scriptures at all if the "men of old" hadn't attuned their inner ears to listen to God. Many of them were not exceptional men, nor were they necessarily spiritual giants. They were simply men who were willing to listen to God, and God, in His faithfulness, instructed them.

Isaiah 65 gives the picture of God desiring fellowship and communication with His creatures:

> I was ready to be sought by
> those who did not ask for me;
> I was ready to be found by those
> who did not seek me,
> I said, 'Here am I, here am I' . . .
> I spread out my hands all the day
> to a rebellious people,
>
> . . . .
>
> When I called, you did not answer,
> when I spoke, you did not listen.

God sent Jesus Christ into the world to repair the broken fellowship between God and man that was caused by man's rebellion and disobedience. Jesus took upon Himself all our sins and guilt so that we can once more stand sinless before a holy and a perfect God.

Anyone who comes to God with no guile in his heart, God will accept as His child. And God will speak to him. It has ever been that way.

"O that today you would hearken to his voice!" (Ps. 95:7). God hears, and He speaks, and I join with the Psalmist who said:

> I love the Lord, because he
>   has heard
>   my voice and my supplications.
> Because he inclined his ear to me,
>   therefore I will call on him as
>   long as I live . . .
> Praise the Lord!
>   (Psalm 116)